Strategies for Preaching Paul

Frank J. Matera

A Liturgical Press Book

THE LITURGICAL PRESS
Collegeville, Minnesota
www.litpress.org

1   2   3   4   5   6   7   8

Library of Congress Cataloging-in-Publication Data

Matera, Frank J.
    Strategies for preaching Paul / Frank J. Matera.
        p. cm.
    Includes bibliographical references and indexes.
    ISBN 0-8146-1966-5 (alk. paper)
    1. Bible. N.T. Epistles of Paul–Homiletical use. 2. Bible. N.T. Hebrews–Homiletical use. 3. Bible. N.T. Epistles of Paul–Criticism, interpretation, etc. 4. Bible. N.T. Hebrews–Criticism, interpretation, etc. 5. Lectionary preaching–Catholic Church. I. Title.

BS2650.55 .M38 2001
251–dc21   00-042840

Contents

For Fr. Michael H. Gosselin
Colleague and Friend

Preface

Nothing is more central to the Church than preaching the gospel. Of this gospel, St. Paul writes in Rom 1:16-17, "It is the power of God for the salvation of everyone who believes: for Jew first, and then Greek. For in it is revealed the righteousness of God from faith to faith, as it is written, 'The one who is righteous by faith will live.'"

Few have preached the gospel with the intensity and insight of St. Paul. In the thirteen letters that the New Testament ascribes to him, the focus of his preaching is the saving work of redemption that God has accomplished for humanity through the death and resurrection of his Son.

It is unfortunate, then, that there is such silence from the pulpit when it comes to preaching from the Pauline texts. Whether it be from lack of familiarity with Paul's theology, or fear of it, preachers rarely preach from his letters, even though he is, perhaps, the most profound writer of the New Testament.

I have written this modest volume to provide pastors with a series of strategies for preaching from the Pauline readings of the Sunday Lectionary. While the work is my own, I am deeply grateful to my colleague in the Department of Theology, Dr. Christopher Begg, who read this manuscript in its entirety, making valuable suggestions for improvement, and to Mr. James Hornecker, a graduate student, for checking scriptural quotations.

Frank J. Matera
The Department of Theology
The Catholic University of America
Washington, D.C.

Introduction

Paul's letters play an important role in the New Testament and in the Roman Lectionary. Of the twenty-seven writings that make up the New Testament, nearly half are attributed to Paul, and, on the Sundays of Ordinary Time, the second reading is usually taken from his letters. Despite the importance of Paul's letters, his teaching is seldom proclaimed from the pulpit.

In part, the explanation for this is that the climax of the Liturgy of the Word is the proclamation of the gospel. Thus the first reading, which is taken from the Old Testament during the course of the Church's Ordinary Time, is meant to prepare the congregation to hear the gospel whereas the second reading belongs to an independent cycle. It is not surprising, then, that preachers focus their homilies on the text of the gospel rather than the readings from Paul.

But if the truth be told, there are other reasons why preachers do not preach from Paul's writings. Among them are the following. First, it is difficult to follow Paul's line of thought because his letters are heard in bits and pieces over the course of several weeks. Even when the preacher sits in the quiet of a study, this remains a problem since Paul is a complicated writer.

Second, even when the preacher has understood something of Paul, it involves a great deal of work to make his theology accessible to contemporary congregations who are familiar with the Gospels but not the epistles. Writing homilies based on Paul's letters, then, requires a great deal of work, and many preachers do not have the time or the will to expend such effort.

Finally, Paul's theology often sounds strange to Catholic ears since Catholics have not been reared on Pauline concepts such as justification by faith, nor does Paul's teaching play the central role in their piety that it does in Protestant piety. Add to this that Paul talks about topics that seem alien and out of date to many contemporary Christians (the second coming of the Lord, the general resurrection of the dead, the need to avoid idolatry) and it is not difficult to understand why there is a great silence when it comes to preaching from the Pauline letters. However, there is no justification for this state of affairs. The silencing of Paul's voice diminishes preaching and deprives the congregation of an aspect of the gospel that Paul presents in a distinctive manner.

This book has been written in the hope of helping to remedy that situation. It is not a technical work, nor is it a substitute for consulting commentaries. Rather, it presents a number of strategies for preaching from the Pauline readings. This book has also been written with a passion for Paul. As I often tell my students, while I believe in Christ, my passion is for Paul. In reading his letters, I encounter someone who has understood how the proclamation of the gospel illumines the human situation and solves the most mundane problems. In reading Paul, I hear someone who has encountered the Risen Lord and knows what it means to live with, for, and in Christ. In reading Paul, I hear a living voice, and it is this voice that I hope to communicate.

This book has been written in view of preaching Paul from the Roman Lectionary, which employs Paul's writings for its second reading most Sundays during Ordinary Time. Thus, during Year A of ordinary time the Church reads from 1 Corinthians, Romans, Philippians, and 1 Thessalonians. During Year B, the Lectionary returns to 1 Corinthians and then reads from 2 Corinthians and Ephesians. Finally, during Year C the Church returns to 1 Corinthians and then reads from Galatians, Colossians, Philemon, 1 and 2 Timothy, and 2 Thessalonians. In effect, the Church reads from all of the letters attributed to Paul except Titus during the course of Ordinary Time, giving special attention to 1 Corinthians and Romans.

To be sure, the Church does not read the whole of any one of these letters, though it does proclaim extended portions of Romans and 1 Corinthians. At the end of the three-year cycle, however, the congregation will have heard a great deal from Paul.

Despite hearing so much, the congregation may be puzzled. Why?

Unlike the congregations to which Paul wrote these letters, contemporary congregations will not have heard these letters within a context of question and answer, problem and solution. Rather, they will have heard one side of what was originally a two-sided conversation. They will have heard Paul's response to questions that the churches posed to him and to problems of which he was aware. Unaware of the original questions and problems of Paul's congregations, and living in a different environment, most contemporary believers will be puzzled by Paul's letters.

If preachers are to preach effectively from Paul, then, they must plan how to proclaim the writings of one of the New Testament's greatest theologians. More specifically, they must acquaint themselves with the background that gave rise to his letters. Why did he write? What questions did he address? What problems did he face? How do his letters respond to these issues?

Historical background, however, is not sufficient. To preach effectively from Paul, preachers must also be aware of the literary structure of his letters and the theological topics with which he deals. Thus, preachers must know how the reading for a particular Sunday fits into Paul's rhetorical and theological argument. When preachers are aware of this, they understand the overall argument and pattern of Paul's letters as well as the development of his theology. They also realize that, while they may not preach from Paul every week, there are periods of two or three weeks when it is opportune to employ the Pauline texts to develop themes such as faith, justification, resurrection, life in community, the power of the Spirit, etc. In other words, preachers need to plan their preaching and decide when and how to preach from Paul.

If this book fulfills its promise, it will help preachers to develop such a strategy. To do this, it will first present the background necessary for understanding the Pauline letter under study. This background study will not be exhaustive or detailed, but it will be sufficient to understand why Paul writes as he does. Next, it will comment on the texts of the Lectionary to show how each functions within the letter. Finally, after examining context and text, this work will summarize the great Pauline themes of the letter in question to highlight the theological dimension of Paul's thought. *Context, text,* and *theology,* then, will be the recurring points in my effort to provide a strategy for preaching Paul.

Paul in Ordinary Time
Year A

During the course of Year A, the Lectionary dedicates eight weeks to 1 Corinthians, sixteen to Romans, four to Philippians, and five to 1 Thessalonians, ample time for any preacher to develop the important themes of these writings. If preachers are to preach effectively, however, they must develop a strategy for determining which texts they will employ and how they will preach from them.

1 Corinthians

1 Corinthians is the only Pauline letter to appear in all three cycles of Ordinary Time. Moreover, it appears at the beginning of each cycle. Thus, in Year A it is read during weeks 2–8, in Year B during weeks 2–6, and in Year C during weeks 2–8. The reason for this, I suspect, is the pastoral nature of 1 Corinthians. More than any other letter, it focuses on a variety of issues such as conflict within the Church, the nature of ministry, marriage, chastity, the danger of scandal, worship, the gifts of the Spirit, death and resurrection, and even money. As the Church begins her Ordinary Time, then, she employs 1 Corinthians to teach what it means to live the Christian life day by day within the community of the Church.

During Year A the readings from 1 Corinthians come from the first four chapters of the letter, except on the Feast of Christ the King when the reading is taken from chapter 15. These four chapters form a neatly defined unit in which Paul resolves pastoral

problems in light of the paradoxical wisdom revealed in the proclamation of the crucified Messiah. Before proceeding to these texts,
however, we must say something about their context.

Strategy: Understanding the Context

Each of Paul's letters has two contexts which preachers
must understand if they hope to preach effectively from his letters. One is historical, the other literary. By the letter's historical
context, I mean the circumstances that occasioned the letter:
why Paul wrote what he did to a particular congregation. By the
letter's literary context, I mean the literary structure of the letter
into which particular texts fit: how Paul wrote in order to instruct, rebuke, and persuade his congregations.

The historical context. According to Acts 18, Paul established a
congregation at Corinth during his second missionary journey
(Acts 15:36–18:22) while Gallio was the proconsul of Achaia
(about A.D. 51–52). After leaving Corinth and visiting Ephesus,
Paul returned to Jerusalem and Antioch and then undertook a
third missionary journey (Acts 18:23–21:14) during which he
spent two years in Ephesus (Acts 19:10). While there, he wrote
a letter to the Corinthians that has been lost (see 1 Cor 5:9).

The Corinthians had also written to Paul (see 1 Cor 7:1),
and some of them even visited him to apprise him of the difficulties besetting his young and immature congregation. Among
these visitors were people from the household of a woman named
Chloe, who told Paul of factions within the community (see 1
Cor 1:11), and a delegation headed by Stephanas, who probably
had a leadership role in the community (see 1 Cor 16:17-18).

1 Corinthians, then, is Paul's response to the reports from
Chloe's people and the delegation led by Stephanas, as well as to
a letter which the Corinthians had sent to him raising questions
about marriage, chastity, the eating of food sacrificed to idols,
conduct in the worshipping assembly, the importance of spiritual
gifts such as prophecy and tongues, the general resurrection of
the dead, and the collection Paul was taking up for the church at
Jerusalem. The historical circumstances that gave rise to the letter
can be summarized in this way:

- Paul establishes the church at Corinth during his second missionary journey.
- While at Ephesus, during the course of his third missionary journey, he writes a letter to the Corinthians.
- Some people from Chloe and a delegation headed by Stephanas inform Paul of a deteriorating situation at Corinth.
- The Corinthians write to Paul about a number of issues.
- In response to the oral reports and the letter he has received from the Corinthians, Paul writes 1 Corinthians from Ephesus.

The literary context. During the course of weeks 2–8, the congregation will hear the following texts: 1 Cor 1:1-3; 1:10-13, 17; 1:26-31; 2:1-5; 2:6-10; 3:16-23; 4:1-5. Heard out of context, few of these texts will resonate with the congregation unless preachers place them within their literary context.

To appreciate the literary context of these texts, it is necessary to understand the structure of 1 Corinthians 1–4 which may be outlined as follows:

1:1-3   Paul's greeting to the church at Corinth.

1:4-9   Paul's thanksgiving for the blessings God has bestowed on the church at Corinth.

1:10–4:21 Paul's discussion of the divisions in the church at Corinth occasioned by the report from Chloe's people and the delegation headed by Stephanas.

    1:10-17   The theme of these chapters and of the entire letter: be united in mind and purpose.

    1:18-25   The theological foundation for Paul's thesis: the weakness and folly of the cross in which God manifests wisdom and power.

    1:26-31   The confirmation of Paul's gospel in the Corinthian congregation whose members are neither wise nor powerful but whom God chose to confound the wise and powerful.

2:1-5	The confirmation of this theme in the ministry of Paul who came to Corinth with fear and trembling.
2:6-16	The nature of the gospel's wisdom which only the mature can understand.
3:1-4	The immaturity of the Corinthians who are in danger of falling into factions because they are attaching themselves to particular apostles.
3:5–4:5	The nature of apostolic ministry.
3:5-9	Ministers of the gospel are God's co-workers.
3:10-17	They must build on the foundation which is Christ.
3:18-23	All ministers of the gospel belong to the Corinthians; it is foolish to attach oneself to a particular minister.
4:1-5	Faithfulness is the most important quality required of a minister of the gospel.
4:6-13	Paul and the other apostolic ministers have endured the ridicule of the world for the sake of the Corinthians.
4:14-21	Exhortation and warning: the Corinthians are not to become inflated with pride.

In 1 Cor 1:10–4:21 Paul has a single purpose: to prevent his immature converts from falling into factions by attaching themselves to any one apostle, be he Cephas, Apollos, or Paul himself. To accomplish this, Paul identifies the crucified Christ as the wisdom of God. Thus, what the world views as folly and weakness (Christ crucified) is the very wisdom of God, and what the world calls wisdom, God views as utter weakness and folly. To prove his point Paul reminds the Corinthians of their election. God did not choose them because they were wise or of noble birth; rather God chose the weak to confound the strong, and the foolish to confuse the wise. Likewise, Paul did not come to Corinth as a powerful speaker but in fear and trembling. The power of his ministry comes from God and not from himself.

The problem at Corinth, then, was a misunderstanding of the gospel's wisdom which only the mature can understand. If the Corinthians understood the paradoxical wisdom of the cross (power in weakness), they would have realized that all the ministers of the gospel belong to them. It is not the individual apostle who is important but God who sent apostles to preach the paradoxical message of the cross. If the Corinthians understood this, they would embrace the sufferings and ridicule that authentic ministers, such as Paul, endure daily for their sake.

Strategy: The Text in Its Context

Once preachers have familiarized themselves with the letter's historical and literary contexts, they are ready to interpret the texts they will preach. In what follows, I will comment briefly on the texts of 1 Corinthians used in Year A in light of what has been said above. My purpose is to show how the texts selected by the Lectionary fit into the historical and literary contexts discussed above.

The Called and Sanctified Community
Second Sunday: 1 Cor 1:1-3

These verses are Paul's greeting to the Corinthians. In them, he announces several themes that he will develop in the letter: his status as an apostle who has been called by Christ Jesus; the dignity of the congregation at Corinth which has been sanctified in Christ Jesus, called to be holy, and is now united with others who call upon the name of the Lord Jesus Christ.

To be called is to be elected as was Israel of old. The election of the Corinthians, however, has taken place in Christ Jesus, in whom the congregation has been made holy. This holiness is God's own holiness which sets the congregation apart and consecrates it for service to God. In this letter Paul frequently exhorts the Corinthians to avoid immorality because they form a sanctified community set aside for service to God. The letter opening, as brief as it is, provides a profound reminder of what the Church is: God's chosen people who have been sanctified by the blood of Christ for service to God, and God alone. In a society that values personal achievement, this might be an opportune time to preach about the Church as a sanctified community which has been chosen and elected by God in Christ. This text affords preachers an occasion to discuss the ethical implications of election: The members of God's sanctified community must become what they have been chosen to be.

Unity of Mind and Purpose
Third Sunday: 1 Cor 1:10-13, 17

This text begins the body of the letter and announces the theme for all that follows in chapters 1–4: Be united in mind and purpose. Paul has been informed that there are rivalries among the Corinthians because they are aligning themselves with the particular apostle who baptized them. In saying that he was not sent to baptize, Paul is not denying the importance of baptism but reminding the Corinthians that they were not baptized into the name of the one who baptized them but into Christ who was crucified for them. This reference to Christ crucified foreshadows Paul's argument that the crucified Christ is the power and wisdom of God.

The opening verses, which call the community to be united in mind and purpose, summarize Paul's theme. Divisions within the community betray the purpose for which Christ was crucified: to unite everyone in one body, the body of Christ. Thus, this week's reading develops the ecclesiological theme broached last week: the called and sanctified community is to be of one mind and purpose because Christ was crucified for it. The focal point of the gospel is Christ, not his ministers.

In a day when the Church is threatened by interest groups and ideologies, and when parishes are in danger of being divided by the same, this text summons contemporary congregations to find their unity in the crucified Christ.

The Foolish, the Weak, and the Lowly
Fourth Sunday: 1 Cor 1:26-31

It is unfortunate that the Lectionary passes over the text of 1 Cor 1:18-25 in which Paul expounds the paradox of the cross: that God manifests his wisdom and power in the weakness and folly of the crucified Christ. If preachers are to make sense of this week's text, they must first immerse themselves in 1 Cor 1:18-25 since it proclaims the central paradox of the gospel Paul preaches.

The text which the Lectionary has chosen is, as my outline shows, a confirmation of this paradox in the life of the community. Taking up the ecclesiological theme of the first two weeks, Paul reminds the Corinthians of their humble origins to show how God elected them. Just as God chose the crucified Christ to manifest his wisdom, so God chooses the foolish, the weak, and the lowly to shame and confound the wise, the powerful, and the haughty.

Believers have nothing of which to boast because their wisdom, their righteousness, their sanctification, and their redemption *is* Christ. Christ is the one who justified them before God; Christ is the one who made them holy before God; Christ is the one who redeemed them for God, because Christ and only Christ is God's wisdom. When contemporary believers boast in themselves and their accomplishments, they contradict the very gospel they claim to embrace.

Ministry as the Work of God
Fifth Sunday: 1 Cor 2:1-5

This text complements last week's reading. Paul employs it to show the Corinthians that God manifests his power in weakness. However, whereas last week's reading dealt with the weakness of the community that was chosen and elected by Christ, this week's points to Paul's own weakness. He did not come to Corinth as an eloquent preacher but in fear and trembling. If his ministry succeeded among the Corinthians, it was because the power of God was at work in him. The success of his ministry, then, rests upon the Spirit of God at work in his ministry.

Continuing the theme of the crucified Christ, Paul says that he resolved to know nothing but Christ crucified, whom he has already identified as God's wisdom and power. When he says that he came proclaiming the mystery of God, he is again referring to the crucified Christ in whom God manifests his power and wisdom. Thus, his gospel is not another form of human wisdom as some of the Corinthians mistakenly believe but the wisdom and power of God.

Ministers of the gospel must never allow their ministry to become a personality cult. Accordingly, preachers might use this text to remind their congregations that faith rests on the power of God rather than the personality and eloquence of the preacher.

God's Hidden and Mysterious Wisdom
Sixth Sunday: 1 Cor 2:6-10

Reference to the mystery of God and human wisdom in last week's reading leads to a further discussion of what Paul means. God's wisdom is Christ crucified: the wisdom and power of God. This wisdom, however, is part of God's mysterious, hidden plan and can only be discerned by the mature. In 2:2-16 Paul identifies the mature as those who are spiritual, by which he means, people who live in the realm of God's Spirit. The Corinthians, however, are carnal because they live in the realm of what is merely human and transitory, as their factions and divisions show. Thus, they have not understood the mysterious and hidden wisdom of the gospel that is Christ crucified.

This is one of the richest texts of 1 Corinthians inasmuch as it points to God's preexistent plan for the salvation of those who believe in Christ. The text, however, must be read in light of what has just been said and what follows. Most importantly, the preacher must never forget that all references to God's wisdom must be interpreted in light of the scandal of the cross.

Preachers might use this text to explain how Christian wisdom stands in sharp contrast to the wisdom of this world. In doing so, it will be necessary to explain that this wisdom is only accessible to those who embrace the crucified Christ and the scandal of the cross.

The Sanctified Community as the Temple of God
Seventh Sunday: 1 Cor 3:16-23

The Lectionary makes use of only one text from chapter 3, but the choice is excellent. In the material which precedes this text (3:1-15), Paul has already compared the Corinthian congregation to a field that the apostles planted and watered but to which God has given the growth. He has also compared it to a building whose firm foundation is Christ Jesus. Paul now employs a third and more powerful image: the community is God's temple because the Spirit of God dwells in it.

The theme of the temple recalls the ecclesiological themes mentioned earlier: the community is God's elect community sanctified in Christ. It also makes one of the boldest statements of the New Testament when it identifies believers as the Temple of God. In effect, Paul says that there is no further need for the Temple of Jerusalem because God dwells among his people in a unique way through Jesus Christ who has sanctified them by his blood. Whereas contemporary Catholics are accustomed to calling themselves the Church, Paul reminds them that they are also the Temple of God.

Having reminded the Corinthians that they are the temple of God, Paul tells them that there is no need to boast of, or cling to, particular apostles such as Apollos, Cephas, or himself. *All* of the apostles belong to the Corinthians. Rather than embrace a particular apostle, they should embrace the paradox of the cross: power in weakness, wisdom in what the world considers folly.

Judgment Belongs to God
Eighth Sunday: 1 Cor 4:1-5

This text concludes Paul's discussion of apostolic ministry. He has argued that true ministers of the gospel are God's co-workers. Now he describes them as servants of Christ and stewards of the mysteries of God. This expression refers to the hidden wisdom of God which is Christ crucified. Everything Paul says is meant to place apostolic ministers in a proper prospective. They play a vital role in the Church, but they are only servants of Christ. The gospel is about the crucified Christ. It is not about them.

Confident of his ministry, Paul is not concerned about human judgment, even if it acquits him. He knows that judgment resides with God alone. He warns the Corinthians, then, that any judgment they make about him is of no account, be it critical or favorable. What matters is his faithfulness to Christ.

Victory over Death
Thirty-fourth Sunday: 1 Cor 15:20-26, 28

The Lectionary makes use of 1 Corinthians one more time during Year A, on the last Sunday of Ordinary Time, the Feast of Christ the King. The text is taken from chapter 15, in which Paul considers two questions. First, will the dead be raised? Second, if they will be, what is the nature of the resurrection body?

The text for this week comes at the end of Paul's teaching about the resurrection of the dead. In this section he argues that there will be a general resurrection of the dead because God raised Christ from the dead, the first fruits of all who have died. In other words, the resurrection of Christ was not an isolated event, *it was the beginning of the general resurrection of the dead.* Because Christ has been raised from the dead, believers can be confident that God will raise them as well. Everything, however, occurs in an orderly fashion.

- Christ is raised from the dead.
- Christ returns at the end of the ages.
- The dead are raised incorruptible.
- Death is destroyed and everything is subjected to Christ.
- Christ hands over the kingdom to his Father.
- Christ subjects himself to God.
- Creation is restored and God is all in all.

This apocalyptic vision provides a breathtaking view of what has happened and what is yet to occur. It is an appropriate reading for the Feast of Christ the King because it shows that Christ is already reigning, and his enemies are being subjected to him. At the present time, Christians live between the resurrection and the parousia. Christ has *already* been raised, but they have *not yet* been raised. When they are raised at the end of the ages, the last and greatest enemy, death, will be destroyed. Then God will be all in all. That will be the moment of final salvation.

This reading is an opportune time for preachers to discuss the nature of Christ's kingship, which is intimately related to the rule of God and ultimately subjected to the Father. It is a time to remind congregations that even though the decisive battle was won on the cross, God's final victory over the power of death has not yet occurred. Without such an understanding of death's power, believers run the risk of thinking that they already enjoy the fullness of salvation.

Strategy: Theological Themes

Preachers need not devote all of their homilies to the Pauline texts we have examined. A better strategy would be to focus on two or three and develop one or two themes. Among the most important are the following.

The Crucified Christ

At the center of Paul's theology stands the cross: the proclamation that God was reconciling the world to himself in Christ (see 2 Cor 5:19). Christ's death on the cross, however, must not be divorced from the proclamation of the resurrection. There are occasions, however, when the scandal of the cross must be brought into the foreground lest Christians revel in a theology of glory that neglects Christ's suffering and death.

Paul found such an occasion at Corinth. His immature congregation was a charismatic community that mistakenly thought it already enjoyed the eschatological salvation reserved for the end of time. Thus, at the beginning of 1 Corinthians, he focuses on the scandal of the cross. By doing so he reminds believers that they cannot rise with Christ until they have died with him. Nor can they participate in the power and wisdom of God until they have accepted the folly and weakness of the cross.

It is the cross which stands as the stumbling block for the world, a sign of contradiction, weakness, and folly. It is the cross that must be preached to remind believers of the mystery of

God that confounds the power and wisdom of the world. When believers understand that God reveals his wisdom in the folly of the cross, they comprehend the wisdom that the gospel brings.

The Elect and Sanctified Community

At several points Paul reminds his congregation that it forms an elect and sanctified community: elect because it has been chosen in Christ; sanctified because it has been washed in the blood of Christ. Because the Church is elected and sanctified, it must maintain a certain distance from the world which evaluates wisdom differently. This is not to say that the Church cannot live in the world. Indeed, it must. But while living in the world, the elect and sanctified community must remember that it belongs to another. It has been set aside and consecrated for service on behalf of the one who was crucified for it.

The Church, then, is God's people, the Temple of God, not because it has chosen to be, or is worthy to be. The Church has been elected and called out of the world through the death of God's Son. The Church has been made holy by the holiness of God whose Spirit dwells in it and makes it a holy temple. When the Church understands its dignity, it strives for the unity of mind and purpose that Paul calls for in 1 Corinthians. Such a Church understands the tragedy of factions and divisions. Such a Church is mature because it lives in the realm of God's Spirit.

Ministers and Servants of the Crucified Christ

Ministers of the gospel play a vital role in building up the Church, if they preach Christ crucified. True ministers of the gospel understand that they are God's co-workers, servants of Christ, and that their primary responsibility is to be faithful to the God who called them.

When the minister becomes more important than the gospel, when style triumphs over substance, when the personality of the minister becomes the foundation for belief, something is wrong. It is no longer Christ who is preached but his minister; it is no longer the gospel that is proclaimed but the preacher.

The proper antidote for immature preachers and immature congregations is Christ crucified, the wisdom and power of God.

Romans

Of the thirteen letters attributed to Paul, Romans is the most important. In addition to being the longest of Paul's letters, it is the most mature statement of the gospel he preached among the Gentiles. It deals with issues of sin, redemption, the Mosaic Law, faith, justification, the Spirit, Israel, and the moral life. Theologically profound, Romans has had a greater influence on the Church than any other New Testament writing. It is not surprising, then, that the Church reads from Romans for a period of sixteen weeks during Year A. What is surprising is the absence of Romans from Year B and C, making it imperative that preachers set aside some time during Year A to preach from this letter so that congregations will hear Paul's teaching on justification by faith apart from doing the works of the Mosaic Law.

Strategy: Understanding the Context

The historical context. When Paul wrote Romans, he had come to the end of his third missionary journey in the Mediterranean basin. Having established congregations in Asia Minor and Greece, he hoped to preach the gospel in the West; that is, he planned to go to Spain. Before preaching the gospel in Spain, however, Paul intended to make two important visits: to Jerusalem, where he would deliver the collection he had been gathering for the poor; and to Rome, a church he had long wished to visit but had been prevented from doing so. Rome would then be the jumping off point for his mission to the West, perhaps with new co-workers drawn from that church to help him in this missionary endeavor (see Rom 15:14-33).

Paul was at Corinth (Rom 16:21-23) when he decided to write a letter of self-introduction to the church at Rome explaining his gospel since there were misunderstandings about the implications of his gospel for sin, righteousness, and the future of Israel. Hints of these misunderstandings are found in texts such as the following.

- And why not say—as we are accused and as some claim we say—that we should do evil that good may come of it? (Rom 3:8)
- What then shall we say? Shall we persist in sin that grace may abound? Of course not! (Rom 6:1)
- What then? Shall we sin because we are not under the law but under grace? (Rom 6:15)
- What then can we say? That the law is sin? Of course not! (Rom 7:7)
- I ask, then, has God rejected his people? (Rom 11:1)

Although these questions are rhetorical, they reflect real objections raised against Paul's gospel by those who did not comprehend his teaching on justification by God's grace through faith apart from doing the works of the Law. Therefore, it was necessary for him to explain that his Law-free gospel does not promote a libertine way of life. To the contrary, it allows "the righteous decree of the law" (Rom 8:4) to be fulfilled in those who believe.

In addition to this ethical issue, Paul's gospel raised questions about the future of Israel and the faithfulness of God. After all, if justification is based on faith rather than on doing the works of the Law, does this mean that God has been unfaithful to Israel? Has God changed the original stipulations of the covenant so as to reject his people? Since an uninformed reading of Paul's writings might give this impression, Paul must show that his gospel does not impugn the faithfulness of God nor does he teach that God has rejected his people. In chapters 9–11, therefore, he takes up the question of Israel's destiny in light of the gospel.

There were, then, at least two issues that Paul needed to clarify before visiting Rome: the implications of his Law-free gospel for the moral life of believers who have been justified on the basis of faith, and the destiny of Israel now that the Messiah has come. In addition to these issues, there was a third, more pastoral in nature: the problem of the weak and the strong described in Rom 14:1–15:13. The problem can be summarized in this way.

The church at Rome consisted of numerous house churches spread throughout the city. While some were composed of Gentile believers who no longer observed the Jewish dietary prescriptions of the Law, others consisted of Jewish believers who continued to observe these prescriptions. Paul was aware of this situation, which was becoming a source of division, and he addressed it toward the end of his letter, referring to the first group as the strong in conscience and the second as the weak in conscience.

To summarize, Paul writes Romans from Corinth at the end of his third missionary journey to clear up misunderstandings about his gospel and to resolve a pastoral problem so that the Romans will receive him when he visits them on his way to Spain.

The literary context. The texts of Romans used in Year A come from chapters 3–6, 8, 9, 11–14. However, preachers should be aware of the manner in which the Lectionary distributes these texts and plan their preaching accordingly. For example, they should note that the Lectionary draws from chapter 8 for five of its readings and devotes two weeks to chapters 5 and two weeks to chapter 11, but only a single week to each of the remaining chapters (3–4, 6, 9, 12–14).

In addition to knowing how the texts are distributed, preachers should have a sense of the letter's overall structure. The following outline should be helpful to most preachers.

1:1-7	An extended greeting in which Paul introduces himself and the gospel he preaches.
1:8-15	A thanksgiving in which Paul expresses his eagerness to visit Rome.
1:16-17	The theme of Paul's gospel: the righteousness of God.
1:18–3:20	A description of human sinfulness which confirms that all have sinned and are in need of God's grace.
3:21-31	The theme of Paul's gospel in light of this sinful situation: the righteousness of God excludes all boasting.
4:1-25	The confirmation of Paul's gospel in the story of Abraham who was justified by faith.
5:1-11	The new condition of those who have embraced the gospel: they are at peace with God, justified, reconciled, hopeful of final salvation.

5:12-21	Christ, the new Adam, whose act of obedience justified sinners.
6:1-23	Freedom from the power of sin.
7:1-25	Freedom from being under the Law which was frustrated by sin.
8:1-39	Life in the Spirit makes it possible to fulfill the just requirement of the Law.
9:1–11:36	God's faithfulness and the destiny of Israel.
12:1–15:13	The moral life of believers justified by faith.
15:14-33	Paul's plans to visit Rome.
16:1-23	Paul's greetings from Corinth to those at Rome.
16:25-27	Final doxology.

Although Romans can be structured in other ways, this outline indicates that the theme Paul develops is the righteousness of God, by which he means God's own righteousness or uprightness, God's faithfulness to himself and his covenant people, God's way of being God, God's reliability in fulfilling his promises. Thus the letter is first and foremost about God–an appropriate topic for any preacher!

The righteousness of God has implications for humans; for in manifesting his righteousness God justifies the sinner, making righteous those who accept his grace in faith. Romans, then, is also about humanity, for it describes the new life of believers who have been justified by God and are now at peace with him, hopeful of final salvation as they live their lives in the realm of the Spirit.

An exposition of the righteousness of God, however, implies a situation of human sinfulness from which humanity cannot extricate itself. Thus Paul must first explain the need for righteousness before he can develop what it means to live a life of righteousness. Why was it necessary for God to send Christ as an offering for sin? What was it about the human condition that made it impossible for humans to do the just requirement of the Law apart from Christ? The answer to these questions requires a fuller exposition of Paul's gospel which will be given as I examine the texts of the Lectionary.

Strategy: The Text in Its Context

During the course of weeks 9–24, the Lectionary makes use of the following texts from Romans: 3:21-25, 28; 4:18-25; 5:6-11; 5:12-15; 6:3-4, 8-11; 8:9, 11-13; 8:18-23; 8:26-27; 8:28-30; 8:35, 37-39; 9:1-5; 11:13-15, 29-32; 11:33-36; 12:1-2; 13:8-10; 14:7-9. While these texts represent a fair amount of Romans, they hardly form a continuous reading whose sense will be immediately obvious to either the preacher or the congregation. It is imperative then that preachers understand how each text fits into its broader literary context.

The Righteousness of God
Ninth Sunday: Rom 3:21-25, 28

This text is the most important text of Romans that preachers will encounter during the coming sixteen weeks. It serves as the theme for all that follows, and preachers must keep its message in mind whenever they preach from Romans.

Romans 3:21-25, 28 is part of a larger unit (3:21-31) which echoes the theme of Paul's letter, the righteousness of God, first announced in 1:16-17:

> For I am not ashamed of the gospel. It is the power of God for the salvation of everyone who believes: for Jew first, and then Greek. For in it is revealed the righteousness of God from faith for faith; as it is written, "The one who is righteous by faith will live."

Between this initial announcement of the righteousness of God revealed in the gospel (1:16-17) and the text of the Lectionary for this week, there is an extended discussion of the human condition which demonstrates that all, Jew as well as Gentile, have sinned and fallen short of God's glory.

The discussion opens with the phrase, "The wrath of God is indeed being revealed from heaven against every impiety and wickedness of those who suppress the truth by their wickedness" (1:18) and proceeds to convict the Gentile world of sin because it has chosen to worship the creature rather than the Creator. Thus, Paul identifies idolatry as the root cause of sin in the Gentile world. After dealing with the Gentiles, he turns his

attention to the Jewish people who have the advantage of knowing God's will through the Mosaic Law and being sealed with
the sign of circumcision (2:1–3:8). He concludes that even
though they were in an advantageous position, they are no better off. For, like the Gentiles whom they judge to be sinful, they
have failed to keep God's commandments.

Paul, then, discloses a situation of universal sinfulness (3:9-
20), which Christians have since called original sin. No one is
righteous before God, not a single person. Moreover, no one
will be justified in God's sight by the works of the Law (3:20),
since it was not the purpose of the Law to justify people before
God but to make them conscious of sin. It is at this point, after
convicting Gentile and Jew of sin, that Paul restates and develops his theme, the righteousness of God.

The righteousness of God, as I have already noted, is
God's own righteousness, his uprightness, his covenant loyalty
to his people, his saving justice, God's way of being God. Thus,
it may be described as a quality of God, and yet it is not an at-
tribute among other attributes. The righteousness of God is
what is most distinctive about God; for it is God's way of effect-
ing salvation. God's righteousness *is* his saving justice for those
who believe in Christ. For those who do not it is wrath, the
theme of 1:18–3:20.

Paul maintains that this saving justice has made its appearance apart from the Law; that is, it does not come from observ-
ing the Mosaic Law. Rather, this righteousness is accessible to all
who entrust themselves to what God has done in Christ rather
than rely upon their own achievements, whatever they be.
Moreover, this righteousness does not contradict what is found
in the Law, for both the Law and the Prophets testify to it. Thus
God has been faithful to Israel since Israel's sacred writings witness to this righteousness.

Because this righteousness does not depend on doing the
works prescribed by the Mosaic Law but on faith in what God
has done in Christ, it is available to all: to Gentile as well as to
Jew. There is no distinction since all have sinned and fallen
short of God's glory. Thus the universal situation of sin that

Paul describes in 1:18–3:20 requires a universal savior accessible to all. That Savior is Christ by whom God freely justifies Jew and Gentile.

The language of justification comes from the law courts and is forensic in nature. Thus, to justify means to acquit or pronounce someone innocent. In this case, God acquits sinners through what he has done in Christ. That acquittal, however, is not a hollow judgment, as though God says, "you are innocent," but nothing has really changed. The righteous judgment of God effects something in the life of believers so that they become a new creation in Christ. Thus, the righteousness of God, God's saving justice, makes sinners righteous and pleasing before God, though it is still possible for the justified to sin again.

In justifying the sinner through what he has done in Christ, God has also redeemed humanity. The metaphor of redemption comes from the social world of Paul where slaves were redeemed by someone who ransomed them by paying for their freedom. In this case, God has redeemed sinners through the blood of Christ, freeing them from the bondage of sin.

Finally, Paul speaks of expiation, a metaphor drawn from Israel's cult, especially the ritual of the Day of Atonement (see Leviticus 16). On that day the high priest entered the inner sanctuary of the temple, the holy of holies, and smeared blood on the cover ("the mercy seat") of the ark of the covenant to expiate or wipe away the sins of the people. Drawing from this image, Paul sees Christ as the new mercy seat smeared with his own blood to cover up or expiate the sins of those who entrust themselves to what God has done in Christ.

Since God has accomplished justification, redemption, and expiation in Christ, no one can boast. A person is not justified before God on the basis of doing the prescriptions of the Law, even the moral and ethical demands of the Decalogue. Rather, justification comes from God as believers entrust themselves to Christ. This is what it means to say that a person is justified by faith in Christ apart from doing the works of the Law.

Preachers will not be able to explain this in a single week. But if they keep this background in mind, they will have something to say about justification by grace through faith in the weeks and months ahead. To be sure the language of righteousness and justification sounds strange to many congregations, but the underlying reality of these terms (God's grace) is not. Paul's teaching on justification proclaims that humanity is utterly dependent upon God for salvation, and nothing believers do is accomplished apart from God's grace.

In a society where the self-made person is still the ideal and economic achievement the benchmark of success, Paul's teaching needs to be heard anew, even if preachers do not employ the technical language of justification.

Abraham: A Man Who Was Justified by Faith
Tenth Sunday: Rom 4:18-25

At the conclusion of chapter 3, after declaring "that a person is justified by faith apart from works of the law" (3:28), Paul asks, "Are we then annulling the law by this faith?" He then answers, "Of course not! On the contrary, we are supporting the law" (3:31). The question probably reflects the kind of objections raised against Paul's preaching among Gentiles. Therefore, if Paul is to commend himself to his Roman audience, he must show that his teaching does not contradict what is already found in Israel's Scripture. To do this, he turns to the story of Abraham.

Abraham plays a central role in the Old Testament, and for the New Testament he is more significant than any other figure of Israel's Scriptures, including Moses. The reason for this is not difficult to explain. While Moses is the central figure of the Old Testament to whom God delivered the Law, it was this Law that separated Israel from the nations. Abraham, by contrast, received a promise that God would make him the father of a multitude of nations. The promise was more inclusive than the Law, a point the early Church was keenly aware of as it fulfilled Jesus' command to make disciples of all the nations.

Aware of the significance of Abraham for his Gentile converts, in chapter 4 Paul employs the story of Abraham to show how he was justified by faith apart from works. His exposition is based upon an exegesis of Gen 15:6, "Abraham believed God, and it was credited to him as righteousness" (4:3). Paul's exegesis proceeds in two stages.

In the first half of the chapter (4:1-12), Paul explains the *second* half of the verse, "and it was *credited* to him as righteousness," focusing on the verb "to credit." In doing so, he shows that righteousness was not *credited* to Abraham's account because of something he had done (the normal meaning of "credit"), but on the basis of his faith in God's promises. In the second half of the chapter (4:13-25), Paul focuses on the *first* half of the verse, "Abraham *believed* God," in order to explain the nature of Abraham's faith. The Lectionary reading for next week will come from the second half of chapter 4, where Paul explains the nature of Abraham's faith.

If preachers wish to grasp what Paul is saying here, they must read this week's text in light of the whole chapter and Paul's stated purpose: to show that God has always justified people (Abraham being the prime example) on the basis of faith rather than works. Thus, Paul's teaching on justification establishes rather than destroys the law.

The text of Rom 4:18-25 recalls the promise God made to Abraham in Gen 17:5: that he would become "the father of many nations" (4:18). When God made this promise, Abraham and Sarah were beyond the age for having children. To use Paul's blunt language, Sarah's womb was dead. Despite the human impossibility of the promise being fulfilled, Abraham trusted because he *believed* that God would fulfill the promise he had made. In effect, Abraham displayed a kind of *resurrection faith*; for, by believing that God could bring forth new life from the dead womb of Sarah, he believed in *the God who raises the dead*. Thus, Abraham did not merely believe in God; he believed in the God who raises the dead, the God and Father of Jesus Christ. This is why God credited righteousness to his account. It was because of his faith in the God who fulfills his promises, even when these promises are seemingly impossible to fulfill. It was not because of anything that the patriarch had done, for not even Abraham can boast before God.

Christians routinely profess their faith in God. But faith in God is not enough! Authentic faith is faith in the God and Father of Jesus Christ; it is faith in the God who raises the dead. Such faith involves more than professing a creed. The faith that justifies is the faith which entrusts itself to God when there is no human reason to hope.

Justified, Reconciled, Saved
Eleventh Sunday: Rom 5:6-11

Chapter 5 is a transitional section. The first half, from which this week's reading comes, summarizes Paul's discussion on justification by faith by describing the present condition of the justified: they are at peace with God; they have access to the divine presence; they are reconciled; and they live in confident hope of salvation. The second half, which will be employed next week, draws a comparison between Adam and Christ to show that just as Adam's transgression led to condemnation for all, so Christ's righteous deed led to universal acquittal. This acquittal results in freedom from sin and Law (chapters 6–7) and affords the justified life in the Spirit (chapter 8).

The Lectionary reading (Rom 5:6-11), then, is part of a larger unit (5:1-11) which begins with a statement that describes the results of justification, "Therefore, since we have been justified by faith, we have peace with God through our Lord Jesus Christ, through whom we have gained access [by faith] to this grace in which we stand, and we boast in hope of the glory of God" (5:1-2). The Lectionary reading, however, begins with v. 6 and focuses our attention on the love of Christ who died for us when we were sinners. Paul employs this language to assure his readers of God's love for them. For, if Christ died for them when they were sinners, they can be even more confident that they will be rescued from God's wrath (see 1:18–3:20) now that they have been justified. Furthermore, if they were reconciled to God when they were still his enemies, how much more confident can they be that they will be saved now that they have been reconciled. The argument moves from the lesser to the greater in this way.

if

while we were still sinners	Christ died for us

how much more confident can we be

that justified by his blood	we will be saved

if

while we were his enemies	we were reconciled

how much more confident can we be

that reconciled through his death	we will be saved

Justification, reconciliation, and salvation summarize what God has done in Christ and what is available to those who entrust themselves to the God who raises the dead. Justification is a forensic term and means that God has acquitted us. That acquittal, however, is no empty declaration, for it results in peace and reconciliation with God. God does not need to be reconciled to humanity, but humanity needs to be reconciled to God. Justified by God and reconciled with him, believers confidently await God's eschatological salvation that will be completed at the resurrection of the dead when death will be destroyed and God will be all in all (see 1 Corinthians 15).

If this text does not resonate with the congregation, perhaps modern life has desensitized people to their profound need to be justified by, reconciled to, and saved by God. Perhaps too many believers take salvation for granted as something due them, too confident that they will be saved. Paul was confident, but his confidence did not rest on anything he had done or accomplished. Unfortunately, the confidence of contemporary believers is sometimes founded on their achievements rather than on what God achieved for them in Christ.

Adam and Christ
Twelfth Sunday: Rom 5:12-15

The second half of chapter 5 presents a comparison between Adam and Christ that has played an important role in the formulation of the Church's teaching on original sin. Though the language of the passage is rather contorted, Paul's main point is summarized in 5:18 which, unfortunately, the Lectionary does not include: "In conclusion, just as through one transgression condemnation came upon all, so through one righteous act, acquittal and life came to all." The one transgression is the disobedience of Adam who transgressed God's command not to eat the fruit of the tree of life. His refusal to obey that command resulted in condemnation for his descendants. The righteous act that resulted in acquittal and life for all is the obedience of the new Adam, Christ, who surrendered himself to death on the cross (see Phil 2:6-11).

What makes this text so difficult to understand is the manner in which Paul interrupts the comparison begun in 5:12 and introduces a number of qualifications before completing it in 5:18. It is as if, having started the comparison, he suddenly realizes that there is no real comparison between these two figures since Christ is so superior. Therefore, he must qualify what he wishes to say by indicating that the gift of God in Christ far surpasses the results of Adam's transgression. Whereas the transgression led to condemnation, the gift leads to acquittal for all.

As difficult as this text is, it is worth preaching from since it deals with one of the fundamental claims of Christian doctrine: the sinful situation of all who are in Adam as contrasted with the grace-filled situation of those who are in Christ. In effect, Paul says that Adam and Christ are the progenitors of two kinds of humanity: sinful humanity and redeemed humanity. And, whether we acknowledge it or not, we are incorporated into one or the other. If we are still in Adam, we live in the realm of sin and death, enslaved to our passions and desires. There is simply no hope for such a humanity; for it is condemned to death. But, if we are in Christ, we live in the realm of grace and the Spirit that will be described in chapter 8. We are no longer slaves to our passions and desires because the power of Christ's Spirit, at work within us, allows us to live in a way pleasing to God.

Those who doubt this should read the newspaper or watch the evening news. The humanity that is still in solidarity with Adam is all too real. It is imperative, therefore, that the Church witness to the new humanity in Christ.

Dead to Sin, Alive to God
Thirteenth Sunday: Rom 6:3-4, 8-11

The baptismal focus of this reading may entice some to say something about baptism. Although this is appropriate, preachers will do well to view Paul's baptismal theology in light of the text's context. This is all the more urgent since this is the only Sunday Lectionary reading from Romans 6–7 during Ordinary Time.

Chapter 6 develops the implications of the Adam-Christ comparison. At the end of chapter 5, Paul writes, "The law entered in so that transgression might increase but, where sin increased; grace overflowed all the more" (Rom 5:20). In saying this, Paul affirms that the effects of Christ's obedience far outweigh those of Adam's transgression. However, Paul seems to realize that his theology can be, and probably was, misunderstood. Therefore, at the beginning of chapter 6, he raises an objection to what he has just said, "What then shall we say? Shall we persist in sin that grace may abound? Of course not!" (6:1; compare 3:8 where Paul proposes a similar argument against his gospel).

Paul is aware that the formulation of his teaching on grace appears to leave little room for the moral life of the believer. If God's grace is stronger than sin, then why not continue to sin, since God's grace will always be more abundant?

However, this is not how Paul would have others interpret his teaching on justification. While it is true that believers are saved by God's grace through faith, the moral imperative to do good remains firmly in place.

It is at this point that Paul introduces his baptismal formula. In doing so he is pointing to the ethical implications of life in Christ. Sin is no longer an option for those in Christ; for, when they were baptized into Christ, they were baptized into his death in order to live a life of obedience to God rather than to sin. Just as Christ's death was a death to sin, so sacramental association with Christ calls believers to die to sin.

In the second part of chapter 6, which the Lectionary does not include, Paul exhorts the Romans not to present themselves to sin but to God. Having been incorporated into the new humanity created by Christ, they are no longer slaves of sin but of righteousness. Thus it is utterly incomprehensible for Paul that anyone who has been baptized into Christ would continue in sin.

Paul, of course, is aware that even the justified can return to a sinful way of life; otherwise he would not spend so much time developing moral exhortations such as this. Such behavior, however, has no foundation in the gospel of grace and justification that he proclaims. To the contrary, this gospel calls believers to the highest moral standards.

This text presents an opportunity to explain the moral implications of the sacramental life. The sacraments, especially baptism and the Eucharist, bring Christians into the closest possible relation with Christ. That relation, however, is not a magical symbiosis whereby believers are assured of salvation no matter what they do. Sacraments call believers to a moral way of life. They summon those who participate in them to a greater righteousness because they have accepted a new lord. Believers no longer present themselves as slaves to sin who can expect the wages of death; for they have become slaves of Christ who produces the fruit of the Spirit, righteousness, in their lives.

Excursus: Preparation for Reading Romans 8

During the next five weeks the liturgy will draw from Romans 8 for its second reading. Since this is the only chapter of any Pauline letter that is employed for five weeks during Ordinary Time, it is evident that the liturgy sees it as important for the Christian life. Accordingly, even if preachers do not preach from these readings, they should become thoroughly familiar with them and the role they play in Paul's theology.

In chapter 5 Paul compared the effects of Christ's obedience with Adam's transgression and concluded that whereas the transgression of the old Adam led to condemnation for all, the righteous act of the new Adam led to justification and life for all. Consequently, those who have been baptized into Christ have died to sin; they are no longer slaves of sin but servants of righteousness. Put another way, incorporated into Christ, they have given their allegiance to a new lord, Jesus Christ.

Incorporation into Christ, however, releases believers from another taskmaster: the Mosaic Law. Thus, in chapter 7 Paul takes up the question of the Law. What he says is almost incomprehensible to most congregations since the Mosaic Law no longer poses the same kind of questions for them as it did to the first Christians who asked: What is the role of the Law now that the Messiah has come?

Paul's answer is complex and still perplexes scholars. The simple answer, however, is found in Rom 10:4, "For Christ is the end of the law for the justification of everyone who has faith." By this succinct statement, Paul means that the Mosaic Law has fulfilled its role in salvation history. Therefore, those who are in Christ are no longer under the Law. Thus Paul writes in Rom 7:6, "But now we are released from the law, dead to what held us captive, so that we may serve in the newness of the spirit and not under the obsolete letter."

If this teaching sounds puzzling, it was also puzzling to many of Paul's contemporaries. After all, the Law was God's gracious gift to Israel. How can Paul say that Christ is the end of the Law, or that believers are no longer under the Law? Such claims would seem to lead to a complete and utter disregard for the precepts of the Law, including the Decalogue. Can there be a moral life, if believers are no longer under the Law? Paul answers this question in Romans 8, but before turning to that chapter it is necessary to say something about Romans 7.

Paul was keenly aware of the difficulties his teaching presented, therefore he raises another objection against his gospel, "What then can we say? That the law is sin? Of course not!" (7:7). In Paul's view, the objection is utterly absurd, and he replies, "By no means!" The real problem, as he will explain, is sin which Paul personifies as a malevolent power. The Law is spiritual and good, and it makes God's will known. However, it does not, and it cannot, give people the power to do what they ought to do. Moreover, sin frustrates the Law's purpose by arousing desire. Thus, when the Law says that one should not covet, sin uses the occasion of the commandment to arouse human desire. Paul expresses the human dilemma in this way,

> So, then, I discover the principle that when I want to do right, evil is at hand. For I take delight in the law of God, in my inner self, but I see in my members another principle at war with the law of my mind, taking me captive to the law of sin that dwells in my members (Rom 7:21-23).

It is at this point that Paul cries out, "Miserable one that I am! Who will deliver me from this mortal body?" (Rom 7:24) and then answers his own question, "Thanks be to God through Jesus Christ our Lord" (Rom 7:25). What Paul means here is explained in Romans 8 which can be outlined as follows:

8:1-4	God has done what the Law could not do.
8:5-8	There is a fundamental opposition between those in the realm of the flesh and those in the realm of the Spirit.
8:9-11	The justified are no longer in the realm of the flesh.
8:12-17	There are ethical and soteriological consequences for this new situation of the justified.
8:18-25	The whole of creation awaits redemption.
8:26-27	The Spirit helps believers in their weakness.
8:28-30	Believers are predestined for glory.
8:31-39	Nothing can separate believers from God's love.

Life in the Spirit
Fourteenth Sunday: Rom 8:9, 11-13

The reading for this week combines two parts of the outline proposed above: the justified are no longer in the realm of the flesh (8:9-11), and there are ethical and soteriological implications to life in the Spirit (8:12-17). The reading however, must be heard in light of the chapter's opening verses, which proclaim that God has done what the Law could not do, and then draw a contrast between those in the realm of the flesh and those in the realm of the Spirit.

What the Law could not do was empower people to observe its requirements. Consequently, it was frustrated by the power of sin. God, however, did what the Law could not accomplish by sending his Son who fully participated in the human condition. However, whereas the first Adam sinned by disobeying God, the new Adam condemned sin by obeying God. Consequently, God accomplished in his Son what the Law could not effect: perfect obedience. As a result of Christ's obedience, it becomes possible for those in him to follow his example through the power of the in-dwelling Spirit.

Paul draws a contrast between those who live according to the flesh and those who live according to the Spirit. The first group consists of those who are still in solidarity with the old Adam. To be in the flesh is to be in Adam, to rely on what is merely human, to put one's trust in what is mortal and corruptible. In contrast to this pitiable situation, those in the Spirit are in the realm of God's Spirit. They have been incorporated into a renewed humanity; they live in Christ and trust in what is immortal and incorruptible. They believe in what they cannot see.

In the reading for this week, Paul reminds his audience that they are not in the realm of the flesh since God's own Spirit dwells in them. He makes this affirmation on the basis of everything he has said thus far about justification by grace through faith. Those who have been justified and reconciled are in the realm of the Spirit, which they have received as a free gift.

This new situation has ethical and soteriological consequences. In terms of the moral life, those who enjoy the gift of the Spirit must live accordingly. It would be an utter contradiction for those in the realm of the Spirit to live as they did when they were in the realm of the flesh. Living in the realm of the Spirit enables believers to do what they could not do under the Law. For the first time they fulfill the Law.

Finally, Paul draws out the soteriological implications of his moral imperative. Life according to the flesh results in death, whereas life according to the Spirit results in life. Here, life refers to life with and for God, whereas death means separation from God.

If this reading is to resonate with the congregation, the preacher must clarify the meaning of life in the Spirit and life in the flesh. It is not a matter of body versus soul, nor should flesh be understood in terms of sexual immorality. Paul is talking about two ways of life: one in solidarity with the old Adam, the other in solidarity with Christ. This is the fundamental choice that lies before every believer: to live in solidarity with Christ empowered by the Spirit, or to live in solidarity with the old humanity enslaved to sin.

The First Fruits of the Spirit
Fifteenth Sunday: Rom 8:18-23

The reading for this week corresponds, for the most part, with the fifth section of my outline (Rom 8:18-25): The whole of creation awaits redemption. The sense of the text will be clearer, however, if preachers read and reflect on the verses immediately preceding this text in which Paul reminds his audience that the Spirit of God has empowered them to call God Father, thereby showing that they are truly children of God and heirs with Christ to the inheritance of glory that God has prepared for them. This glory is participation in God's own life.

At the present time believers live in a world that does not correspond with the redemption they experience through the power of God's Spirit. Although they are children of God and call God Father, they live in bondage to corruption and decay as a result of sin. Consequently, believers must endure a troubling tension in their lives: on the one hand, they live in and by the Spirit. On the other, they live in a world that has not yet been set free from the ravages of sin.

Aware of this, Paul portrays creation as waiting for the eschatological glory to be revealed in the children of God. When that occurs, creation will be set free. Put another way, at the present time the world does not see and cannot acknowledge the glory which has already been revealed in believers through the power of God's Spirit. When this glory is finally revealed, creation will be set free. Thus, Paul's vision is one of total redemption that includes creation as well as humankind. In this vision, he views believers as the beginning, the first fruits, of a glory yet to be revealed.

This text offers preachers an occasion to present their congregations with a vision of salvation that includes the whole of creation. Creation must be set free from the effects of Adam's transgression. That process has begun in the Church, where the Spirit of God has made believers children of God. Since this will not be completed until what has happened in the Church includes the whole of creation, it is imperative for believers to understand their role in God's plan. They are the first fruits of redemption and must live accordingly.

The Spirit, the Source of Strength
Sixteenth Sunday: Rom 8:26-27

The text for this week consists of only two verses; therefore it is important for preachers to understand its context before deciding how to preach from it.

Thus far, Paul has shown that the Spirit of God enables believers to do what the Law commanded but could not enable them to do: to observe its just requirements. Reminding the Romans that they live in the realm of the Spirit, Paul calls them to live according to the Spirit. Next, he reminds them that they are the first fruits of a glory yet to be revealed which will affect all creation. Therefore, it is necessary for believers to live in hope and patience for what they do not see: the glory yet to be revealed.

In this time of hope and waiting believers are weak, for they live in a creation that is frustrated by the power of sin. Their weakness makes it difficult to pray to God as they ought. However, the Spirit comes to their rescue. Just as the Spirit enables them to carry out the just requirements of the Law, so it enables them to pray as they ought.

Prayer is one of the most common experiences of Christians. Teaching people how to pray effectively, however, is one of the most challenging of all pastoral duties. To be sure, people can and should be taught the basic prayers of the Christian life. The kind of prayer of which Paul speaks here, however, goes further; for, it envisions God's own Spirit making intercession on behalf of the believer. Whether such prayer is personal or communal, it is always effective since it is guided by God's Spirit who knows God's will.

Although teaching believers to pray in and by the Spirit requires a more extended ministry than a homily, the homily is an excellent occasion to remind congregations that the Spirit plays a vital role in their prayer life. Left to our own devices, we do not know how to pray to God who is mysterious and beyond our comprehension. When we live in the Spirit, however, the Spirit empowers us to pray.

Called, Justified, and Glorified
Seventeenth Sunday: Rom 8:28-30

This reading summarizes the great themes that Paul has been developing in the first eight chapters of this letter (election, justification, glorification). Its major premise, which will be developed further next week, is that everything works to God's purpose. Consequently, believers can be confident that all things work for good for those who love God. To explain this, Paul establishes a verbal chain that moves from predestination to election to justification to glorification.

The most difficult of these concepts is predestination, which gives the impression that God has predestined some for salvation and others for damnation. This is not Paul's meaning. Writing from the vantage point of one who has been chosen and elected, Paul realizes that what has happened to him and others is part of a larger plan: God's purpose for creation. Therefore, he says that believers have been predestined for glory by being conformed to the image of God's Son, the eschatological Adam.

Understood in this way, Paul does not mean that God has chosen certain people and rejected others. Rather, Paul employs this language to remind believers that their election, justification, and glorification did not occur by chance. It is part of God's purpose.

If preachers are willing to struggle with the thorny concept of predestination, this text provides an opportunity to remind congregations that their election is part of God's eternal plan of salvation. The justified have been called because God has predestined them for glory. But what about those who have not been justified? Are they predestined to damnation? The text does not address this question since it has a different purpose: to remind the justified that they have been predestined for glory.

Preachers would do well to focus on what the text says and re-serve other questions for adult education sessions.

No Separation from God
Eighteenth Sunday: Rom 8:35, 37-39

This text is the dramatic conclusion of the first eight chap-ters of Romans. It begins with a simple question ("What will separate us from the love of Christ?") and concludes with Paul's firm conviction that nothing can separate us "from the love of God in Christ Jesus our Lord."

The love of Christ and the love of God in Christ Jesus is to be understood as the love of Christ and the love of God for us, rather than our love for God or Christ, though this is not excluded. Paul's question can be phrased in this way: Is there anything that can separate us from the love that God has for us in Christ?

Why would Paul ask such a question? What he has been saying in chapter 8 provides a clue. At the present time, as they wait for final glory, believers find themselves in a period of suf-fering and tension. The world does not recognize them, and they do not recognize the world. In such a period of trial, even believers might wonder if God still loves them. With his escha-tological vision of what God has in store for those whom he has chosen, Paul assures his audience that nothing in this world, or beyond this world, can separate them from God's love.

It is difficult to preach a text such as this to a congregation that is complacent and self-assured. In moments of trial and tribulation, however, it is one of those texts that makes eminent sense. Thus, the text can be used to comfort or disturb the con-gregation, as occasion demands. The preacher will comfort those in distress, and disturb those who have lost all fear of being separated from God because they are secure and comfort-able in their present circumstances.

Excursus: Preparation for Preaching Romans 9–11

For the next three weeks the Lectionary employs a series of texts from Romans 9–11. Since it is important to read these texts in light of their context, preachers should reflect upon them as a unit before trying to preach from them.

In these chapters Paul takes up another objection to his gospel, one that is relevant to the Church given the ever-recurring temptation to anti-Semitism: the question of Israel's destiny. More specifically he refutes the charge that his gospel to the Gentiles implies that God has rejected his people (11:1).

This objection was undoubtedly raised by some who misunderstood Paul's preaching. For, if a person is justified by grace through faith, rather than on the basis of doing the prescriptions of the Mosaic Law, does this not imply that God has changed the rules? Put another way, has the God who made the covenant with Israel at Sinai been unfaithful to his people by requiring faith rather than works?

Chapters 9–11, however, are not merely about Israel; they are about God. Or to return to the theme of this letter, they are about God's own justice and uprightness, his faithfulness to his covenant promises. If the gospel that Paul preaches among the Gentiles means the rejection of Israel, it would mean that God has been unfaithful to Israel. More importantly, it would mean that God has not been faithful to himself.

Although Paul's answer to this objection is straightforward, it is also quite subtle. The immediate answer is that God has not rejected his people. Indeed, believers like Paul are proof of this, for Paul is "an Israelite, a descendant of Abraham, of the tribe of Benjamin" (11:1) who believes that Jesus is the Messiah. The more subtle answer is that not all Israelites belong to Israel, and not all of Abraham's children are his descendants (Rom 9:6-7). Rather Abraham's true descendants are those who believe in the promise of God (Rom 9:8) and rely on the righteousness that comes from God.

Having made this point, Paul affirms that after the full number of the Gentiles has entered the Church, Israel will be saved (Rom 11:25-26). Paul does not explain how or when this will happen because the present hardening of Israel's heart is a divine mystery. He is absolutely confident, however, that God will show mercy to the members of his people who have not yet believed.

These chapters have important consequences for the Church and its relation to the Jewish people. Although the Jewish people do not believe in Jesus as the Messiah, they remain God's chosen people. God has not rejected them, nor are they responsible for the events of Jesus' death that occurred two thousand years ago. The Jewish people remain central to God's plan, and in God's own way and time, they will be saved.

There is no place for anti-Semitism among those who believe in Christ. To be anti-Semitic is to curse the heritage that comes through Israel. During the next three weeks preachers might consider preaching about God's enduring faithfulness to Israel and the horror of anti-Semitism.

Paul's Abiding Love for his People
Nineteenth Sunday: Rom 9:1-5

These are the opening verses of Paul's discussion about Israel. To make sense of them preachers should read the whole of chapter 9 in which Paul employs his election theology to proclaim the mercy of God. The present unfaithfulness of Israel does not mean that God is unjust, though it may seem unjust (from a merely human point of view) that God has chosen some rather than others. No one can find fault with God who chooses whom he chooses. To do so would be as foolish as a piece of pottery arguing with the potter who molded it.

The real problem does not lie with God but with certain members of Israel who have trusted in their physical descent from Abraham rather than in God's promises. Were they to trust in those promises, they would be among the elect as well. As Paul explains at the end of chapter 9 and throughout chapter 11, they strove to establish their own righteousness rather than rely on the righteousness that comes from God, "For Christ is the end of the law for the justification of everyone who has faith" (Rom 10:4).

Preachers will not be able to explain all this in a single homily, but they can focus on Paul's concern for his people and remind their congregations of Israel's privileges: adoption as the children of God, the covenants, the Law, the temple worship, the promises, their ancestry. In doing this, preachers will communicate the Church's concern for the Jewish people who remain God's chosen people.

God's Gifts Irrevocable
Twentieth Sunday: Rom 11:13-15, 29-32

Since this week's reading comes from two parts of chapter 11, preachers will do well to reflect on the whole of chapter 11. The chapter begins with the question Paul has been addressing: "has God rejected his people?" (Rom 11:1). Paul answers "no." Rather, the entrance of so many Gentiles into the new faith will eventually make Israel jealous and lead to repentance. There is a danger, however, that the Gentiles will lord their new situation over Israel. Therefore, Paul warns them not to become proud. If they do, they will find themselves in the same situation as unbelieving Israel. To make this point Paul introduces the parable of the olive tree (Rom 11:17-24). Shortly after this, he reminds his Gentile audience that God's gifts are irrevocable. Just as the disobedient Gentiles received mercy, so disobedient Israel will receive mercy.

This text provides another opportunity to speak about the danger of anti-Semitism. Christianity is not an entirely new religion; it is the daughter of Israel. Though the majority of contemporary Christians are of Gentile lineage, their faith arose out of Israel. The task of the preacher is to remind the congregation of its relation to the Jewish people, a relation which needs healing and understanding.

The Unfathomable Mystery of God
Twenty-first Sunday: Rom 11:33-36

Read in isolation, this text is an acclamation of God's unfathomable mystery. Read in context, it is the conclusion to Paul's reflection about the destiny of Israel.

Having stated his understanding of what has happened to his people, Paul ultimately abandons himself to the divine mystery: God's judgments are inscrutable and his ways unsearchable. When all is said and done, humans cannot understand the ways of God. Thus, after the most sophisticated theological reflection, the wise acknowledge that they do not know. Acknowledging this, they trust in the one whom they cannot comprehend.

We do not know why the Jewish people did not accept Jesus as the Messiah. We do not know how and when they will be saved. However, we believe that God is upright and will not reject his people. How, why, and when are not for us to discern. There are moments when only silence, praise, adoration, and faith will suffice. If believers learn this, they will attain wisdom.

Excursus: Preparation for Reading Chapters 12–14

The final three Lectionary readings from Romans come from 12:1–15:13, a section that is best described as moral exhortation. Since the Lectionary only reads selections from these chapters, it is important to read these texts in light of their literary context.

These chapters play an important role in the argument that Paul has been developing, for they show that the gospel he preaches among the Gentiles calls believers to the highest ethical standards. The end of the Mosaic Law does not mean the end of morality. Thus, in Romans 12 Paul calls the community to unity and love, reminding them that they are the body of Christ. In such a community there is no place for revenge or retaliation, either toward the members of the community, or toward those outside of the community.

In Romans 13 Paul takes up a practical matter: the payment of taxes to Rome. Somewhat confidently, he asserts that all authority comes from God, and believers should willingly pay the taxes that are due the Roman state. One wonders what Paul would have said in the face of a blatantly evil regime such as Nazi Germany.

Finally, in 14:1–15:13 Paul takes up another matter, a dispute between certain members of the community. He identifies one group as weak in conscience because it abstains from certain foods and observes certain days as holy (Jewish believers) and the other as strong in conscience because it does not (Gentile believers). Although this moral exhortation does not provide a systematic statement of Paul's moral vision, it suggests how believers should live in community.

The Moral Life as Worship
Twenty-second Sunday: Rom 12:1-2

These verses begin Paul's moral exhortation and summarize what the Apostle believes about the moral life of believers; namely, the moral life is an act of worship. Thus believers should present their bodies as a living sacrifice to God. They should be transformed by the renewal of their minds rather than be conformed to the world.

To understand what Paul means here it is important to recall the picture of human depravity described in Romans 1. In that chapter Paul accused the Gentiles of being senseless because their *minds* were darkened by sin (Rom 1:21), and of degrading their *bodies* by following the lusts of their hearts (Rom 1:24). Conformed to the world, sinful humanity could not offer God the spiritual worship proper to God.

Justified and reconciled believers find themselves in a new situation. At peace with God and made alive by God's Spirit, they can offer themselves to God as a spiritual sacrifice for the first time. Thus their moral life is an act of worship. In this new dispensation, believers worship God when they live in accordance with the Spirit of God rather than in accordance with the flesh.

Although this is a brief text, the theme of transformation in Christ provides preachers with an opportunity to explain the nature of the moral life of believers. When believers live in accordance with the urging of that Spirit, their lives are an act of worship. When they do not, they are in solidarity with the old Adam and conform themselves to the sinful world from which Christ redeemed them.

Love the Fulfillment of the Law
Twenty-third Sunday: Rom 13:8-10

This reading comes immediately after Paul's exhortation: "pay to all their dues, taxes to whom taxes are due, toll to whom toll is due, respect to whom respect is due, honor to whom honor is due" (Rom 13:7). Having told his audience to pay what they owe, he instructs them that their deepest debt toward each other is love for one another; for, love is the fulfillment of the law. Preachers will do well to read what precedes this text since Paul says a great deal about love and non-retaliation in Romans 12, themes which echo Jesus' Sermon on the Mount.

What Paul says about love also echoes what Jesus says about the commandment to love one's neighbor (Matt 22:39). Such love is the fulfillment of the Law. Once more Paul's gospel requires believers to live a deeply moral life, and the key to this moral life is the love commandment. Thus, those who love their neighbor will fulfill the deepest meaning of the Law.

It is not unusual for believers to proclaim that love fulfills the Law. The question that arises, however, is the nature of this love. For Paul love is the self-sacrificing love that Jesus manifested when he gave himself for our sins upon the cross. Preachers must communicate what Paul and Jesus mean by love, when they proclaim that love is the fulfillment of the Law. Romans 12, with its exhortation not to retaliate or seek vengeance, will assist them in this regard.

Belonging to the Lord
Twenty-fourth Sunday: Rom 14:7-9

These verses come in the midst of Paul's discussion about the weak and the strong (14:1–15:13), and preachers will do well to read them within that context. Read in this way, it is evident that believers cannot do whatever they want, even if their conscience convinces them that a particular action is not harmful (as was the case with the strong who had no scruples about what foods they ate). Believers live within the community of the Church, and not all are at the same level of understanding. Therefore, there are times when they must restrain even their legitimate rights less they offend the weaker members of the community.

More importantly, believers belong to the Lord who has died for them. Their lives are not their own. Indeed, our lives are never our own. We always belong to someone or something, for good or for ill. Since those who are in Christ belong to him, it is imperative that they act as servants of the Lord rather than as masters of their own lives.

Contemporary American society extols those who are in control of their lives; such people are the masters of the universe. While control over one's life may be desirable, it is not what the Christian life is about. Preachers may have to disturb their congregations by reminding them of what they do not want to hear: their lives belong to another. Those who accept this message will find a new freedom in their service to Christ.

Strategy: Theological Themes

Romans is filled with powerful theological themes. Among the most important are the sinful situation of humankind in Adam, the justification and reconciliation God has effected in Christ, the importance of living by faith, the enabling power of God's Spirit, and the faithfulness of God.

The Sinfulness of Humankind in Adam

American society boasts of its optimism and confidence in human progress. It believes in progress and is confident that the future will be better than the past. Thus, it is difficult for Americans to understand why there is evil in a society as technologically advanced as their own. Human progress should have long since eliminated such failure.

Paul, however, knew that the human situation was not a problem to be mended by human progress; for he understood that apart from Christ humanity lives in solidarity with the old Adam. Apart from Christ, humanity lives under the power of sin, a power unleashed by Adam's transgression and ratified by every sin thereafter. In other words, Paul knew that humanity has been infected by what later theology would call original sin.

Paul understood that the power of sin is so pervasive that it frustrates the purpose of God's Law and cripples the best of human intentions. Human beings may know what they ought to do, but apart from Christ they cannot do it. Thus it was necessary for God to send his Son in the flesh to redeem humanity from this sinful situation.

American society needs to be reminded of Paul's realism about sin. It needs to be reminded that apart from Christ humanity lives in solidarity with the old Adam whose end is death. While such preaching may seem negative and pessimistic to some, Christians call it realism, a constant reminder that humanity lives in a world where the power of sin is ever present.

Justified and Reconciled in Christ

Although Christians are realistic about the presence of evil in the world, they are hopeful about the future. Their hope, however, is founded on what God has done in Christ rather than in human progress. Christians believe that God has already acquitted them. They no longer stand before God's tribunal condemned but as a people whom God set free and whose lives have been transformed.

Justified by God, Christians are at peace with God because God has reconciled them to himself. The enmity that resulted from Adam's transgression has been overcome, and now humanity has access to God in Christ.

Once more Christians are realists. Although they have been justified and reconciled, they know that they have not yet been saved. Thus the correct answer to the bumper sticker, "Are you saved?" is "Not yet." Final salvation is reserved for God's eschatological victory over death. It is enough for believers to know that they have been justified and reconciled by God's grace through Jesus Christ. Such knowledge frees them from a naive optimism based on human progress and the despair that comes when confronted with the power of sin.

Living by Faith

While American society encourages people to live on the basis of what they see, hear, and feel, the gospel calls those who have been justified to live by faith. More specifically, it calls people to live by the faith that characterized the life of Abraham who believed in the God who raises the dead.

It is not sufficient to believe. After all, everyone believes in something, even if it is only the myth of human progress. But

Christians believe in the God of Jesus Christ, the God who raises the dead. They entrust themselves to the God who justifies them in and through Christ. They believe in the power of God to redeem them.

Such faith must not be reduced to intellectual assent, though it includes such assent. Rather, it is faith that entrusts itself to another just as spouses entrust themselves to each other, and children entrust themselves to their parents. This faith believes that God can and will effect what he promises, and this makes all the difference.

Empowered by God's Spirit

For Paul, life can be viewed in one of two ways. Either one lives according to the flesh, or one lives according to the Spirit. To live according to the flesh is to hope and rely on what is human, corruptible, and mortal. It is the way that a good part of American society lives when it defines life in terms of material goods. Preachers, then, might explain the phrase "living according to the flesh" in terms of the materialism and consumerism that affect much of contemporary American life, even the lives of believers.

In contrast to this way of life, living according to the Spirit means relying on what is incorruptible and immortality; it is reliance on the unseen God. It is another way of talking about the life of faith. Those who live according to the Spirit live in the realm of God's Spirit which enables them to do what they could not otherwise do. They live in solidarity with Jesus Christ. The Spirit makes all the difference.

Except for small pockets of charismatic believers, it often seems that the power of the Spirit has been extinguished in most parishes. Consequently, the Spirit seems to be a concept more than a reality. Preachers will do well to show their congregations where and how the Spirit is already at work in their lives and encourage them to fan that flame into a consuming fire.

The Righteousness of God

Romans is a letter about the righteousness of God: God's integrity, God's faithfulness to his people, God's way of righting what is wrong. The lesson that must be heard repeatedly is that God does not always act as we might expect. As Abraham discovered and Paul learned, God is the God who justifies the ungodly.

The abiding theme of Romans is this righteousness, the faithfulness of God. In calling Gentiles to righteousness through faith, God did not reject the Jewish people. In justifying those who believe, God has been utterly faithful to his promises. Ultimately, the gospel is about the God who acts in and through Jesus Christ. Authentic preaching will focus on this theme and proclaim it again and again.

Philippians

The Lectionary draws upon Paul's Letter to the Philippians four times during the course of Year A: 1:20c-24, 27a; 2:1-11; 4:6-9; 4:12-14, 19-20. Except for the second text, which contains the famous Christ hymn, these readings are brief and do not provide us with the full scope of the letter. Consequently, if preachers are to make sense of them for their congregations, they must read and reflect upon the whole letter.

Strategy: Understanding the Context

The historical context. Philippians is classified as one of Paul's captivity epistles because the Apostle writes from prison (see Phil 1:7, 13, 14, 17). The place of his imprisonment, however, is a matter of dispute. While many favor the period of his Roman imprisonment (early 60s), others argue that the letter was written at an earlier period when Paul was imprisoned at Ephesus or Caesarea (mid to late 50s). Whatever the answer, it is important for preachers to know that Paul writes from prison as he awaits the outcome of a trial that may result in his death.

Despite these trying circumstances, the mood of this letter is one of quiet confidence. Paul is at peace with himself, and he is confident that no matter what happens to him, it will promote the proclamation of the gospel. Thus, despite his present circumstances and the prospect of death, there is a tone of confidence and joy in this letter.

The Philippian community was especially dear to Paul, and it had recently sent him a gift of money to support him during the period of his imprisonment. The gift was delivered by Epaphroditus who then returned to Philippi with this letter in which Paul thanks the community for its gift (Phil 2:25-30; 4:15-20). In addition to thanking the community for its gift, Paul encourages the Philippians to make his joy complete "by being of the same mind, with the same love, united in heart, thinking one thing" (Phil 2:2).

To assist them in becoming a united community, he points to the example of Christ, as described in the Christ hymn. Moreover, he points to the example of his own life as a model worthy of imitation. Thus, he writes, "Join with others in being imitators of me, brothers, and observe those who thus conduct themselves according to the model you have in us" (Phil 3:17).

To summarize, Philippians is a letter of thanksgiving and moral exhortation: thanksgiving for the community's monetary support; and moral exhortation to live in unity and peace after the example of Christ and Paul.

The literary context. There has been a rather vigorous debate about the literary unity of Philippians among New Testament scholars because of the change in tone that occurs in 3:1–4:1, where Paul warns the community of outsiders who seek to impose their Jewish way of life on the Philippians. Others, however, argue that the letter is a literary unity with a unifying theme. In my view, they are correct.

Philippians begins with a traditional letter opening (1:1-2) and then moves to a section in which Paul thanks God for the community's partnership in preaching the gospel (1:3-11). After this thanksgiving, he describes his circumstances (1:12-26) and, on the basis of his behavior in trying circumstances, he exhorts the community to unity (1:27–2:18). He then informs them that he will send Timothy and Epaphroditus to them (2:19-30) and warns them of outsiders who might try to compel them to live a Jewish way of life (3:1-21). Finally, he appeals for reconciliation between two women, Euodia and Syntyche (4:1-9), thanks the community for its support (4:10-20), and concludes the letter (4:21-23).

The overarching theme of Philippians, then, can be summarized in this way. Participation in the ministry of preaching the gospel calls people to participate in Christ's sufferings. Those who participate in these sufferings imitate the example of Christ and Paul.

Strategy: The Text in Its Context

While it is always important to read a text within its literary context, this is especially true for the Lectionary readings taken from Philippians. For, even when these texts are read consecutively, they do not give a full sense of what the letter is about. Thus it is necessary to interpret and reflect upon these texts within their literary context.

Consumed by Christ
Twenty-fifth Sunday: Phil 1:20c-24, 27a

This text occurs within a unit in which Paul explains his circumstances to the Philippians (1:12-26). He is in prison, but his imprisonment has benefited the gospel by encouraging others to preach Christ. Although some preach from selfish ambition and increase Paul's suffering, he is not disturbed since Christ is being preached. Encouraged by the prayers of the Philippians, he continues to rejoice, confident that he will be delivered. But even if he should be condemned to death, Paul remains confident that whatever happens to him, Christ will be exalted.

Paul has arrived at a profound insight about his apostolic life: neither life nor death can separate him from Christ nor impede the preaching of the gospel. The gospel will be proclaimed even if he is put to death. Indeed, his death may even cause it to flourish all the more.

In relating his circumstances, Paul presents himself as a model for the Philippians, who are experiencing community divisions, to imitate. This is why the Lectionary ends with a verse that is actually the beginning of a new section, "Only, conduct yourselves in a way worthy of the gospel of Christ" (1:27). If the Philippians want to know what Paul means, they should look at the example of Paul who has attained peace and joy in prison as he awaits a sentence of life or death.

Those who preach from this text should provide their congregation with the background necessary to understand it. If they do, they can show their congregations that the ultimate success of the gospel does not depend on human effort, for there is no chaining the Word of God. Moreover, for those who have embraced the wisdom of the gospel, there is a God-given peace and joy in the most trying circumstances.

The Example of Christ
Twenty-sixth Sunday: Phil 2:1-11

This is the most important text of Philippians. Also proclaimed on Palm Sunday, it has played a central role in discussions about Christ's preexistence. Paul, however, employs the text for moral exhortation, assuming that his congregation is familiar with the hymn's profound theology. Contemporary preachers will do well to follow his lead.

The text is part of a larger unit, the moral exhortation of 1:27–2:18, in which Paul calls the community to unity. However, whereas he earlier presented himself as an example to be imitated (1:12-26), now he presents Christ as a model to be imitated.

The passage falls into two parts. The first (2:6-8) begins with the exaltation and abasement of God's preexistent Son who did not regard equality with God as something to be grasped at. Rather, even though he enjoyed a divine status, he became human and humbled himself to the point of dying a death reserved for slaves, crucifixion. Thus, though he was the Son of God, Christ humbled himself in the most humiliating way known to the Roman world.

In the second part of the passage (2:9-11), Paul develops the movement from abasement to exaltation. Because the preexistent Son humbled himself in this manner, God exalted him by giving Jesus the divine name, "Lord." This is why the whole universe must confess that Jesus Christ is Lord.

The pattern of self-abasement and exaltation that Paul establishes in this text is similar to Jesus' teaching in the Gospels:

the first will be last, and the last will be first, the greatest is the servant of all. It is the fundamental paradigm of the Christian life but the most difficult to learn. If the Philippians adopt this pattern in their lives, they will make Paul's joy complete and live as a united community.

Factions and divisions have always been part of church life and will continue to be so. The gospel, however, calls believers to conform their lives to the model of self-abasement exemplified by Christ. Those who imitate him will do nothing from self-ambition, nor will they consider themselves better than others. Such people will be exalted by God and live peacefully in community.

Living without Anxiety
Twenty-seventh Sunday: Phil 4:6-9

This brief reading comes at the end of Philippians, in a section in which Paul calls his two co-workers, Euodia and Syntyche, to reconciliation (4:1-9). Having asked them to set aside their differences, he calls upon the entire community to rejoice because the Lord is near. Paul's conviction that the parousia of the Lord is close at hand forms the basis for what he says in this text: there is no need to worry or to be anxious; the Philippians should pursue what is true, honorable, just, pure, pleasing, and commendable. If the Philippians have any doubt about what Paul means, his final words should dispel it: "Keep on doing what you have learned and received and heard and seen in me" (4:9).

These words introduce the theme of imitation that is so prominent in Philippians. Christ is the primary example for believers to imitate, but if they need help in imitating him they can look to Paul who has so conformed himself to Christ that he calls others to imitate him.

While preachers can develop the theme of imitation in terms of Christ and the saints, they should also remind the congregation of its responsibility to provide an example for others to imitate. Having imitated Christ and the saints, believers must be ready to say, "imitate us, and you will know what it means to live in and for Christ."

The Secret of Being Satisfied
Twenty-eighth Sunday: Phil 4:12-14, 19-20

This text comes from the final part of Philippians (4:10-20) in which Paul thanks the community for the monetary support it sent with Epaphroditus. Paul enjoyed an especially warm relationship with this community, and it had aided him during the early days of his mission in northern Greece (4:15). The arrival of the community's gift, now that Paul is imprisoned, was further evidence of the community's concern for him.

The passage reveals an apostle who has grown in wisdom through the many hardships he has suffered. Although he is grateful for the community's gift, the rigors of his ministry and the experience of imprisonment have taught him to live with equanimity in times of abundance and of need. Moreover, he has learned that he can do all things through Christ who has strengthened him. In effect, the imprisoned Paul has become a model of what it means to live in good and bad circumstances.

This text speaks to a consumer society that prizes the comfortable life and a superabundance of wealth. Americans live either in abundance or in need, but only a few know the secret of living with both. Preachers should remind their congregations that peace does not come from an abundance of material goods anymore than a lack of such goods can deprive one of peace. The secret of peace is living with one's circumstances, especially when they cannot be changed and are beyond one's control.

Strategy: Theological Themes

Philippians presents preachers with two theological themes: self-effacement and imitation. Both must be understood within the broader context of life in community.

Self-effacement

The self-effacement of which Philippians speaks is rooted in the kenosis or self-emptying of Christ who did not consider his divine status something to be taken advantage of during the period of his earthly life. By an act of self-effacement that made him the servant of others, he emptied himself to the point of dying an ignominious death on the cross. The self-effacement of which Philippians speaks, therefore, is an act of service on behalf of others for the sake of building up the community.

A concept such as this is foreign to contemporary western society which encourages people to promote themselves and be all they can be. It only makes sense within a community of like-minded believers who confess that their Lord is the servant of all. In such a setting, the self-effacement of Christ becomes the key to living in community with one mind and one heart.

Imitation

The one theme that occurs in all of the Lectionary readings from Philippians is imitation: imitation of Christ and imitation of Paul. This theme is deeply rooted in Catholic piety as mediated by Thomas à Kempis's *The Imitation of Christ* and Butler's *Lives of the Saints*. Unfortunately, it has been neglected in recent years, and secular society now provides many believers with other examples to imitate, usually sports and entertainment figures.

It is important, therefore, for preachers to recover the theme of imitation. Imitation is Paul's way of speaking about discipleship and can be summarized in this way. Believers imitate Christ by imitating the pattern of his obedient life-giving death on the cross. They participate in Christ's death to the world with the firm hope that God will raise them from the dead, just as he raised his obedient Son. Because Paul has so identified himself with the pattern of Christ's death and resurrection, he calls others to imitate him so that they can imitate Christ. In effect, he provides his congregations with a model of what it means to die and live with Christ. People are always in need of examples to show them what it means to live in and for Christ. Contemporary believers should become such examples and patterns for others to imitate.

1 Thessalonians

1 Thessalonians, the earliest writing of the New Testament, was composed around A.D. 50–51, less than twenty years after

Jesus' death. The Lectionary employs this letter at the end of the liturgical year because of its teaching on the Lord's return, what the New Testament calls the parousia.

Strategy: Understanding the Context

The historical context. Paul founded the Thessalonian congregation during the course of his second missionary journey. Having been called in a vision to preach the gospel in Greece (Acts 16:9-10), he and Silas went to Philippi (Acts 11:12) and then to Thessalonica to preach that Jesus is the Messiah (Acts 17:3). Although he was able to establish a small congregation there, those who refused to believe in the gospel drove him out of town. From Thessalonica, he went to Beroea (Acts 17:10), Athens (Acts 17:15), and Corinth (Acts 18:1). Concerned about his congregations, Paul sent Timothy to Thessalonica to survey the situation. On the occasion of Timothy's return, Paul wrote 1 Thessalonians from Corinth, where he had now settled.

Overall, Timothy's report was positive. In writing 1 Thessalonians, therefore, Paul's purpose was to strengthen the congregation in its faith since the community was experiencing a certain social dislocation because it had adopted a faith that others considered threatening and subversive. Consequently, in this letter Paul employs moral exhortation to remind the community of what he had already taught and to encourage its members to live in accordance with the faith they had embraced.

Closely related to this moral exhortation is Paul's teaching on the Lord's parousia. The Thessalonians were concerned that believers who had already died would not share in the victory of the Lord's parousia, for they mistakenly thought that only the living would be taken up at the parousia. Paul uses the occasion of this letter to teach that those who have believed in Christ will share in his victory at the parousia, even if they have died. Moreover, throughout the letter he reminds the Thessalonians of Christ's imminent return in order to motivate them to live in accordance with the gospel.

The literary context. 1 Thessalonians has two parts. The first (chapters 1–3) is an extended thanksgiving in which Paul thanks

God for the faith, hope, and love of the community. The second (chapters 4–5) is an extended moral exhortation in which he reminds the Thessalonians of what he has already taught about the moral life and exhorts them to live holy and blameless lives as they prepare for the return of the Lord who will rescue them from the coming wrath of God.

A number of themes appear in both parts of the letter. Among the most important are the following: (1) God has called, chosen, and elected the Thessalonians for salvation; (2) The new life of the Thessalonians is one of faith, hope, and love; (3) The Thessalonians have imitated Paul and become an example to others; (4) The Thessalonians have been called to holiness and must flee immorality; (5) The Lord's coming is imminent, therefore the Thessalonians must be holy and blameless on the day of the Lord.

The Faith, Hope, and Love of God's People
Twenty-ninth Sunday: 1 Thess 1:1-5b

This reading consists of Paul's greeting to the Thessalonians and the first part of the letter's thanksgiving which will be concluded in next week's reading. In his greeting, Paul identifies the Thessalonians as a congregation rooted in God the Father and Jesus Christ the Lord. Such language should remind contemporary congregations that their very existence depends upon what God has done in Christ; namely, God has chosen and elected them. The theme will appear several times in 1 Thessalonians and occurs at the end of this reading when Paul reminds the congregation that it has been chosen by God.

To understand the power of this statement, it is important to recall that one of the prerogatives of ancient Israel was its election. Israel was not to be like the Gentiles because God had chosen Israel to be his special people, more beloved than all the nations of the earth. In this letter Paul applies that prerogative to a group of recent Gentile converts who, only a few months earlier, had worshiped idols.

The Thessalonians now enjoy the prerogatives of Israel. They can say that they are God's people because God is their

Father and Jesus Christ is their Lord. They now live a life characterized by faith, love, and hope. In speaking of faith, love, and
hope, Paul writes in a way that may sound strange to those familiar with Romans and Galatians; for he speaks of their *work* of
faith, their *labor* of love, and the *steadfastness* of their hope. What
he means is the work that *is* faith, the labor that *is* love, and the
steadfastness that *is* hope. The Thessalonians manifest these
qualities in their lives because Paul's gospel has come to them in
the power of the Holy Spirit who is active in the community.
Paul exhorts them, "Do not quench the Spirit" (5:19), for it is the
life-force of the community which lives by faith, hope, and love.

This reading provides preachers with an opportunity to remind their congregations that they have been chosen in Christ.
The Church is a people who have been called out of darkness
and sin to be God's people. It is not an intentional community
in the sense that a group of people decide to make themselves
the Church but a community which God has chosen, and to
whom God has given life through the Spirit. Such a community
lives a life of faith in Christ who is Lord, of love for the other
members of the community (see 4:9-12), and steadfast hope that
Christ will come again.

Imitators of Paul and Models for Others
Thirtieth Sunday: 1 Thess 1:5c-10

This reading is a continuation of the thanksgiving prayer
on behalf of the Thessalonians begun last week. In his thanksgiving prayers Paul often announces themes that will be developed in the rest of the letter, for example, the theme of election.
In this portion of the thanksgiving, he highlights two other
themes: imitation and the imminent return of Christ.

The imitation theme is already familiar to us from Philippians. However, there is a new element here: through their imitation of Paul the Thessalonians have become a model for other
believers throughout Macedonia and Achaia (Greece). The
Thessalonians became a model for others when they turned
from idols to serve the living God and await the return of his
Son. The gospel required a profound change in their lives which

alienated them from the society in which they lived. No longer willing to worship idols, they now serve a God whom their contemporaries do not acknowledge. Moreover, their lives are founded on the hope that the Son of God will rescue them from a fearful judgment when he comes again.

It is difficult for contemporary believers to appreciate the change that faith in Christ required of those first Christians. Christianity was not an acceptable way of life, for it was perceived as a danger to established society, especially to the family. Paul was aware of this and did his best to remind his converts that they belonged to a new family which transcends their earthly family: God's elect people. Those in Christ are brothers and sisters to each other. Preachers might employ this text to remind their congregations that Christianity was not always perceived as an acceptable religion.

Working Night and Day
Thirty-first Sunday: 1 Thess 2:7b-9, 13

With this reading, Paul returns to the theme of imitation by presenting himself as a model for the Thessalonians to imitate. To appreciate this text, it should be read in the wider context of 2:1-12, in which Paul reminds the community of his behavior. Although shamefully treated at Philippi, he still had the courage to preach the gospel. He was not deceitful but spoke to please God. He did not flatter them, nor was he greedy. Rather, he was as gentle as a nursing mother, and he supported himself by working night and day. He dealt with them as a father with his children, encouraging them to live a life worthy of the God who called them. Accordingly, the pattern of Paul's life becomes an example for them to imitate.

A text such as this might seem like boasting to contemporary congregations. To make sense of it, preachers may have to explain that Paul's purpose is to present himself as a model for imitation. In doing so, preachers might ask themselves what kind of person presents himself so confidently for other to imitate? The answer is simple: one who has conformed himself to Christ!

Christ Will Come Again
Thirty-second Sunday: 1 Thess 4:13-18

In the final weeks of Ordinary Time, the Lectionary draws from two readings that focus on Christ's parousia. Both occur within the second part of the letter (4:1–5:24) in which Paul presents the congregation with an extensive moral exhortation to live a life worthy of their election as they wait for the Lord's coming. Paul encloses his discussion of the parousia with two moral exhortations, thereby highlighting the intimate relationship between the moral life and hope in the parousia.

4:1-13	A*n exhortation* to live a life of holiness and love.
4:14-18	The relationship between the Lord's *parousia* and the resurrection of believers.
5:1-11	The need to be vigilant because the *parousia* will occur unexpectedly.
5:12-24	*An exhortation* regarding life in community.

The Thessalonians expected Christ to return during their lifetime. When members of their community died, and the Lord did not return, they asked, "What will happen to the dead at the Lord's parousia? Will they share in the Lord's victory, or will they miss out?" Today's reading is Paul's response to that question, a question which may sound strange to many contemporary believers who rarely think of the Lord returning in their lifetime.

Paul's answer is clear. There is an intimate connection between the resurrection of Christ and the resurrection of those who believe in him. At the parousia the dead will be raised and be with the Lord forever. In fact, they will be in an even more advantageous position than those who are still alive because they will be raised first. Then the living will be taken up with them to meet the Lord.

This is a difficult reading to preach because it must make use of images and symbols to describe something that has not yet occurred: the return of the Lord and the resurrection of the dead. The preacher's task is complicated since few Christians believe that the Lord will return in their lifetime. The Lord's parousia, however, is the faith which believers proclaim every week, "Christ has died, Christ is risen, *Christ will come again!*" What, then, does it mean to proclaim the resurrection of the dead and the Second Coming of the Lord?

Two points need to be made here. First, the resurrection of Christ is not an isolated event: it is the beginning of the general resurrection of the dead. It is the beginning of the end time. Because Christ has been raised, believers will be raised. The general resurrection, however, will not occur until the end of the ages when Christ will return. However, the fact that Christ has already been raised means that he can return at any moment to inaugurate the general resurrection of the dead.

Second, Christ's parousia is God's final victory over sin and death. The definitive victory was won on the cross, but the powers of sin and death will not be destroyed until the parousia when the dead will be raised and death destroyed. Thus, the parousia is God's final victory, and this is why the Church confesses "Christ will come again."

A beginning point for preaching this text might be the eucharistic acclamation or the statement of the Creed, "he will come again to judge the living and the dead." A reflection on these statements, which the congregation professes each week, will show how central the parousia is to Christian faith.

When Christ Will Come Again
Thirty-third Sunday: 1 Thess 5:1-6

Having explained the intimate connection between the resurrection of Christ and the resurrection of all believers, Paul turns to the question of time: When will the parousia occur? Paul himself thought that he would be alive when the Lord returned (see 4:17). That was also the expectation of the Thessalonians, some of whom were probably engaged in speculation as to when Christ would return.

As confident as he is that Christ will return, Paul is aware that he does not know when this will happen. Therefore, lest the Thessalonians try to divine when Christ will return, he reminds them that the parousia will occur at a moment they least expect.

Thus Paul calls upon the community to do the one thing they can in such circumstances: be vigilant. It is more important to live as children of the light than to know the exact time of the Lord's return. It is more important to shun the darkness than to speculate about the Lord's return.

While Paul faced a situation in which it was often necessary to calm the apocalyptic expectations of his congregations, most contemporary preachers face a different problem: hope for the return of the Lord plays little or no role in the lives of many Christians. There is no sense of urgency in their lives, no expectation that God's power can break into their lives at any moment.

Contemporary preachers must help their congregations understand what it means to proclaim that Christ will come again. To do this, they might explain that the presence of sin and evil in the world shows that God's final victory has not yet taken place. There is still something to hope for, a final redemption that Christ will effect in God's own time. Such hope requires believers to live with an awareness that they are in profound need of the final salvation that only God can effect in Christ.

Strategy: Theological Themes

Although brief, 1 Thessalonians is rich in theology. Among its most important themes are election, imitation, the call to live a life of holiness, the imminent coming of the Lord, and the triad of virtues that characterize the new life of believers (faith, hope, and love). The Lectionary, however, has chosen to read Thessalonians at the close of the liturgical year because of its teaching on the parousia. Therefore, this theme, more than any other, should occupy the attention of preachers.

Parousia is the transliteration of a Greek word that means "presence," but it is often used in reference to the return of Christ at the end of the ages when he will function as God's eschatological agent. The firm conviction that Christ will come again is central to Paul's theology, this leading to the question: Was Paul wrong? In my view, Paul was mistaken, but he was not wrong. He was mistaken inasmuch as Christ did not return in his lifetime, but he was not wrong in his central conviction that Christ will come again and play a decisive role in God's final victory.

The challenge of preaching 1 Thessalonians is learning to rethink the eucharistic acclamation, "Christ will come again." Understood in a merely literal manner (Christ coming on the clouds of heaven), the teaching makes little sense to most contemporary believers. However, the teaching makes eminent sense when preachers proclaim that the final act of salvation has yet to take place, and when it does Christ will play the central role. In effect, the parousia assures the Church that it has a future which belongs to God and his Christ.

Paul in Ordinary Time
Year B

During the course of Year B, the Church reads from the following Pauline letters: 1 and 2 Corinthians, and Ephesians. The Letter of James is also read, as is the Epistle to the Hebrews, and on the Feast of Christ the King the reading comes from the book of Revelation. Although Paul did not write the Epistle to the Hebrews, I include it in my discussion of the Pauline letters since certain parts of the early Church viewed it as Pauline. Moreover, since Hebrews is among the most theologically sophisticated writings of the New Testament and also occurs in Year C, preachers should be familiar with it.

1 Corinthians

Chapter 1 has already provided a general background to 1 Corinthians, and there is no need to repeat that material here. The following remarks will focus on historical and literary issues of which preachers should be aware.

Strategy: Understanding the Context

The historical context. 1 Corinthians is a reply to an oral report that Paul received about the community as well as his response to a letter the community sent to him. Generally speaking, the first six chapters of the letter are Paul's response to the oral report, and the remaining chapters are his reply to the letter he received from the Corinthians.

The oral report raised two issues: the problem of factions and divisions within the community (1 Corinthians 1–4) and the problem of sexual immorality (1 Corinthians 5–6). The reading for the Second Sunday of Ordinary Time (1 Cor 6:13c-15a, 17-20) comes at the end of this discussion about immorality.

The letter that Paul received from the Corinthians raised a number of questions about marriage, divorce, and virginity (1 Corinthians 7); participation in cultic banquets at which the food had been sacrificed to idols (1 Cor 8–11:1); worship within the community (1 Cor 11:2–14:40); and the resurrection of the dead (1 Corinthians 15). The readings for the Third and Fourth Sundays of Ordinary Time are part of Paul's response to the community's letter that dealt with questions of marriage, divorce, and virginity, while the readings for the fifth and sixth Sundays deal with the issue of participation in banquets that involve the worship of idols.

The literary context. In addition to this historical background, preachers must be aware of the literary context in which each text is found. Since the texts of 1 Corinthians for Year B occur in three different literary contexts, I will comment upon each.

In 1 Cor 5:1–6:20 Paul deals with three issues: the case of a man living in concubinage with his father's wife (5:1-13); the problem of believers bringing lawsuits against each other in civil court (6:1-8); and the continuing problem of immorality among certain members of the community (6:9-20). Though these issues may seem unrelated to each other, a common problem underlies each. The immature Corinthians have not understood what it means to be a sanctified community because they have not comprehended the wisdom of the gospel: Christ crucified.

Because the Corinthians have not understood what it means to be a sanctified community, they have not expelled the immoral man from their midst, and they have allowed non-believers to judge their lawsuits rather than settle them themselves. Finally, because they have not understood what it means to be a sanctified community, some are still engaging in immoral behavior. The theme that runs through chapters 5–6 can be summarized in this way: those who belong to the sanctified community must avoid immorality.

The opening verse of chapter 7 indicates that this is the beginning of Paul's response to a letter from the Corinthians: "Now in regard to the matters about which you wrote." Paul then quotes from that letter, "It is a good thing for a man not to touch a woman" (1 Cor 7:1).

Chapter 7 suggests that in addition to immoral people, there were people of a more ascetical temperament at Corinth who were urging married couples to abstain from sexual relations. Although Paul freely chose to live a celibate life, he did not impose this kind of life upon others, for he viewed his way of life as a gift. Moreover, he was hesitant about encouraging married couples to abstain from sexual relations lest they succumb to immorality. Consequently, he allowed married couples to restrain from sexual relations for a time if they could do so without falling into immorality, but he did not command it.

After discussing abstinence and conjugal relations, Paul deals with a number of issues concerning marriage. His lively hope in the parousia plays an important role in his discussion. He reasons that since Christ is about to return, it is best for believers to remain as they are. Consequently, he advises widows to remain unmarried unless they cannot practice self-control (7:8-9, 39-40), and he instructs virgins to remain as they are, if they can, but he does not forbid them to marry (7:25-38). In sum, Paul grounds his teaching in Christ's parousia. Since Christ will return soon, believers should remain in the social condition in which they were called, for the world as they know it is passing away (7:17-24).

In 8:1–11:1 Paul deals with another issue raised by the Corinthians, "meat sacrificed to idols" (8:1). The issue arose because some members of the community continued to participate in cultic banquets even after becoming Christians. Participation in these banquets was important for the social life of most Corinthians since they were held in connection with marriages, funerals, and business contracts. Convinced that idols have no real existence, some believers saw no difficulty in participating in these cultic banquets. Those whose consciences were more delicate, however, were scandalized by such behavior. In his response, Paul counsels the strong in conscience to refrain from participating in these banquets lest they offend the weaker members of the community for whom Christ also died. He warns the strong that their confidence may lead them to fall into idolatry, as did Israel of old.

In chapter 9 Paul describes his apostolic ministry as marked by the selfless surrender of legitimate rights for the sake of the community. Thus, he presents himself as a model for the Corinthians to imitate. The material of chapters 8–10 forms a chiasm.

8:1-13   *Admonition* not to participate in banquets where the food has been sacrificed to idols.

9:1-27   *The example of Paul* who has sacrificed his legitimate rights as an apostle for the sake of others.

10:1–11:1   *Admonition* not to participate in banquets where idols are worshiped lest one fall into idolatry.

The central part of the chiasm highlights the example of Paul's life and presents it as a solution to the problems confronting the Corinthians. Imitating his apostolic example, the strong should sacrifice their own rights for the sake of the weak.

Strategy: The Text in Its Context

The Body Belongs to the Lord
Second Sunday: 1 Cor 6:13-15a, 17-20

This text belongs to Paul's discussion about immorality which began with his judgment of the man living with his father's wife (5:1-13). After instructing the community to expel the immoral man from the sanctified community, Paul takes up the question of lawsuits (6:1-8) and then, in this section, exhorts the community to avoid sexual immorality (6:9-20).

Paul begins this unit (6:9-20) by reminding the Corinthians what they were before their conversion. They were immoral people until they were washed, sanctified, and justified in the name of Jesus Christ and in the Spirit of God (6:11). But now they are a sanctified community because of what has been done in them through Christ and the Spirit.

Believing themselves beyond the ordinary rules of moral conduct, some members of the community were employing slogans such as "Everything is lawful for me" (6:12) to excuse their immoral behavior. They believed that just as the stomach is meant for food, so the body is meant for sexual activity. These immature believers saw no contradiction between their immoral way of life and the new life they were called to live in Christ. It is at this point that Paul reminds them that their bodies are not meant for fornication since they belong to Christ. Their bodies are members of Christ's body, and it is inconceivable to Paul that they would surrender them to immoral behavior.

Paul concludes with a strong admonition that the Corinthians are to shun immoral behavior. His reasoning is profoundly theological: their bodies are no longer their own. They were purchased at the price of Christ's blood. The body of each believer is a temple of the Holy Spirit.

Although the Lectionary text does not include the Corinthian slogan, "Everything is lawful for me" (1 Cor 6:12), this would be a good place to begin since it captures the ethos of many Americans who believe that their body is their own to do with whatever they wish. Such an approach to body ethics contradicts the gospel since believers belong to the one whose death washed, sanctified, and justified them. This is the proper starting point for sexual ethics within the sanctified community.

Living as If
Third Sunday: 1 Cor 7:29-31

This brief reading belongs to Paul's discussion about marriage, divorce, and virginity which was occasioned by the letter he received from the Corinthians. Although we do not know what the Corinthians wrote, it seems that an ascetical group within the community wanted others, even married couples, to abstain from sexual relations. While Paul approves of celibacy, he understands that not every one can embrace it. Therefore, his advice is practical: remain in the state in which you were called. If you were married when you became a believer, remain married; if you were not, do not seek a spouse. But if you do, you do no wrong.

Paul's reason for this advice is the substance of this week's reading: "the time is running out . . . For the world in its present form is passing away" (7:29, 31). By these phrases, which begin and end the reading, Paul indicates that the Lord's coming is at hand. Therefore, believers should not alter their social status.

Given this background, it may seem more difficult than ever to preach from this text. After all, while the Christian community firmly believes that Christ will come again, few believe that the parousia will occur in their lifetime. It is precisely this attitude, however, that this text addresses. For, even if the parousia does not occur in our lifetime, our life will end, and we will stand before the judgment seat of Christ. To live *as if* our life will never end is the height of folly, whereas to live with the knowledge that our life will end is the beginning of wisdom.

Free from Anxiety
Fourth Sunday: 1 Cor 7:32-35

This reading may be offensive to some married couples, but it may also resonate deeply with others. It may be offensive to some inasmuch as it describes husbands and wives as divided in their allegiance to the Lord. On the one hand, they want to please the Lord; on the other, they want to please each other. But the text may also resonate deeply with many other married couples who understand just how difficult it is to live the Christian life in trying and difficult circumstances, especially when one spouse does not believe with the same fervor as the other. Therefore, it is important for preachers to approach the text with care.

First, a warning! Although Paul extols the life of celibacy, he does not do so at the expense of marriage. A careful reading of 1 Corinthians 7 shows that he is defending the marital rights of spouses against a group who would deprive married couples of these rights. Second, Paul realizes that celibacy is a gift, and only those who can exercise self-control should embrace it. Freely embraced as a gift, it frees one from anxiety. Third, Paul writes in light of the parousia. He would like the unmarried to remain as they are, if they can, because the time is short, and the end will bring trials and difficulties. In such circumstances the unmarried will have an advantage.

The point of the text is devotion to the Lord. Paul wants people to be free from those daily anxieties that prevent them from serving the Lord with devotion. While the unmarried should be free from such anxieties, too often they are not. And while marriage does produce its share of anxieties, the married life of those who live in Christ remains an authentic expression of the Christian life.

Surrendering Legitimate Rights
Fifth Sunday: 1 Cor 9:16-19, 22-23

This reading belongs to the central section of Paul's discussion about participation in banquets at which the food has been sacrificed to idols (8:1–11:1). On first reading it may appear that chapter 9 has little to do with this question, but this chapter is the central part of a chiasm in which Paul points to his own life as an example of what it means to sacrifice one's rights for the sake of others.

At the end of chapter 8, after encouraging the strong not to offend the weak by attending sacrificial banquets, Paul writes, "Therefore if food causes my brother to sin, I will never eat meat again, so that I may not cause my brother to sin" (8:13). Thus Paul establishes the principle that he will sacrifice even his legitimate rights for the sake of communal unity.

In chapter 9 Paul develops this principle. He insists that he is free. He has the right to be accompanied by a wife, and he has the right to be supported by the Corinthian community. Nevertheless, he has surrendered these rights for the following reasons. First, an obligation has been placed on him to preach the gospel, for Christ has pressed him into service as his apostle. Consequently, though compelled to preach Christ, he preaches free of charge to show that he acts freely. Second, though free, Paul has made himself a slave to all, so that by becoming all things to all, he might save some for Christ. Thus Paul presents himself as an example to the Corinthians of what it means to surrender one's rights for the sake of others.

In a society in which individuals insist on their rights, Paul's words may sound strangely counter-cultural. Why would anyone make himself or herself the slave of others? Why would anyone try to become all things to all people? Such a person sounds like someone without principle or purpose. Paul's solution makes little sense to those who believe that the rights of the individual supersede the common good. Within the community of the Church, however, his example should make eminent sense. For if the Church is the body of Christ, then the strong must take into consideration the needs of the weak.

Imitating Paul
Sixth Sunday: 1 Cor 10:31–11:1

This week's reading is the conclusion of Paul's discussion about participating in banquets where the food has been sacrificed to idols. Throughout this discussion he has argued that the strong must not offend the weak, even if their conscience convinces them that they may participate in such banquets. In the course of this argument, he points to the example of his apostolic ministry; for he has relinquished many of his legitimate rights in order to preach the gospel more effectively. Having made this point, Paul concludes with the bold statement, "Be imitators of me, as I am of Christ" (11:1).

Although the theme of imitating Paul occurs frequently in his letters (see 1 Cor 4:16; Phil 3:17; 1 Thess 1:6), it may sound like boasting to contemporary congregations. However, it did not sound so strange to Paul's converts who had not seen the Lord as had Paul. If they were to imitate Christ they needed a model, and Paul provided it. This is why he says, "Be imitators of me, as I am of Christ." Paul had so conformed himself to the crucified Christ that he could write, "I have been crucified with Christ" (Gal 2:19).

While all Christians are called to imitate Christ, those who preach the gospel have an obligation to model the gospel for others. They should be able to stand before their congregations and say, "imitate me, as I imitate Christ." Or, congregations should be able to say, "we imitate those who preach the gospel to us, because their lives demonstrate what it means to be crucified with Christ." If neither preacher nor congregation can say this, something is wrong. This text provides preachers with an opportunity to consider anew the theme of imitation.

Strategy: Theological Themes

In my consideration of the Lectionary readings for 1 Corinthians during Year A, I mentioned the theme of the sanctified community. Year B develops this theme further by warning believers to flee immorality because they have been washed, sanctified, and justified in Christ. In addition to this theme, Year B presents the theme of imitation which also plays a prominent role in the Philippian readings of Year A.

Likewise, the readings of this year provide preachers with an opportunity to broach the topic of chastity from a new vantage point: body ethics. Although believers are free, their bodies are not their own. Sexually immoral behavior is always inappropriate for those who belong to Christ.

2 Corinthians

The presence of both 1 and 2 Corinthians in Year B means that more than 40 percent of the second readings in ordinary time this year come from Paul's Corinthian correspondence. 2 Corinthians, however, is different in tone and content when compared with 1 Corinthians, nor is it as well known. The tone of this letter is more personal as Paul spends a great deal of time defending his apostolic ministry to a congregation which has become mistrustful of him. Whereas the Corinthians were on trial in 1 Corinthians, it is Paul who is on trial in 2 Corinthians.

Strategy: Understanding the Context

The historical context. 2 Corinthians supposes a lively interaction between Paul and the Corinthian community that can be summarized as follows. At the end of 1 Corinthians, Paul informed the Corinthians that he intended to visit them, and perhaps even spend the winter with them (1 Cor 16:5-9). When Paul finally came to Corinth, his visit proved disastrous, and he refers to it as a painful visit (2 Cor 2:1) because someone caused him great pain (2 Cor 2:5). Exactly who this person was and what happened, we do not know, but he deeply offended Paul, and the community did not come to Paul's defense.

As a result of this incident, Paul returned to Ephesus and did not spend as much time at Corinth as he had promised. This led the Corinthians to criticize Paul severely. When he returned to Ephesus, therefore, Paul wrote a harsh letter "out of much affliction and anguish of heart" (2 Cor 2:4), that he dispatched through Titus. We no longer possess this letter.

Anxious to learn how the community received his letter, Paul left Ephesus and went to Troas in hope of meeting Titus. Not finding him there, he traveled to Macedonia (2:12-13), where he finally met Titus. Titus reported that the harsh letter resulted in the community's repentance (7:5-16) and the punishment of the person who had offended Paul (2:5-11).

From Macedonia Paul wrote the letter we now call 2 Corinthians. More complex than 1 Corinthians, this letter is Paul's most personal correspondence, sometimes conciliatory in tone, other times rebuking and defensive. It is little wonder, then, that some argue that the present form of the letter is a compilation of several Pauline letters assembled by a later editor. Fortunately, preachers need not deal with this issue, though being aware of it may help them to understand the sudden shifts of mood and tone within the letter, especially between chapters 1–9, where the dominant theme is reconciliation, and chapters 10–13, where Paul vehemently attacks a group of outsiders whom he sarcastically dubs "super-apostles."

The literary context. While it is important for preachers to understand the historical background to Paul's letters, it is also crucial that they appreciate how each letter coheres as a literary unit. This is especially so for 2 Corinthians whose literary structure is not immediately obvious to most readers.

The letter falls into two parts: chapters 1–9, from which the Lectionary draws seven of its eight selections, and chapters 10–13, which contains the eighth Lectionary text. In the first nine chapters Paul discusses his apostolic integrity and the glory of his apostolic ministry which is revealed in weakness and suffering. After this profound reflection on his apostolic ministry, he summons the community to be reconciled to God and to himself. He then encourages it to complete the collection begun a year earlier for the church at Jerusalem.

In chapters 10–13 Paul's mood becomes harsher as he defends himself against outsides who have criticized him to the Corinthians. After defending himself against these "super-apostles" (11:5), he warns the Corinthians to mend their ways before he comes for his third and final visit. In these chapters, Paul develops the paradox that is so central to his gospel: *God's power is made perfect in weakness.* Consequently, he boasts in his sufferings and weaknesses as an apostle because he knows that when he is weak, then he is strong! By contrast, the super-apostles foolishly boast in those things that show their power and strength. In doing so, they unwittingly deprive themselves of the power that comes from Christ. Alfred Plummer outlines the letter in this way.

1:1-11   Greeting and thanksgiving for God's consolation.
1:12–7:16 A review of Paul's recent relations with the community.

> 1:12–2:17   Why he postponed his promised visit and sent the harsh letter.
> 3:1–6:10   The glory of Paul's apostolic ministry on behalf of the new covenant despite the sufferings he endures as an apostle.
> 6:11–7:16   An appeal to the Corinthians to be reconciled.

8:1–9:15   An exhortation to complete the collection for the church at Jerusalem.
10:1–13:10 Paul's defense against his accusers.

> 10:1-18   His apostolic authority.
> 11:1–12:18 His foolish boasting.
> 12:19–13:10 Final warnings in view of his impending visit.

13:11-13   Conclusion.

Strategy: The Text in Its Context

Paul's Integrity
Seventh Sunday: 2 Cor 1:18-22

The Corinthian community called into question Paul's integrity because he had changed his travel plans. Instead of visiting them twice, as he promised, he returned to Ephesus after a very painful visit to Corinth. This week's text occurs in a section of the letter that explains why he altered his travel plans; namely, after that painful visit, he decided not to visit them again, lest another visit result in an even more painful situation (see 1:15-16, 23, and 2:1).

In the course of defending his integrity, Paul draws upon the example of Christ's integrity. Christ's response to God was wholehearted when he obediently surrendered his life on the cross. His response was not "yes" one moment and "no" the next; it was a total and unequivocal "yes." For this reason all of God's promises find their fulfillment in Jesus Christ.

In a remarkably bold move, Paul draws a comparison between his integrity and the integrity of Christ. Just as Christ was complete in his allegiance to God, so Paul is complete in his commitment and love for the community. He did not change his travel plans because he was fickle but because the community was not prepared to receive him as it ought.

Integrity is always in short supply, and most people find ways to compromise what they believe without calling their dissimulation a lie. In a world that desperately thirsts for integrity, Paul's example provides a model for contemporary believers who ought to make the example of Christ the basis of their own integrity, as did Paul.

A Letter of Recommendation
Eighth Sunday: 2 Cor 3:1b-6

This reading begins a section in which Paul provides the Corinthians with a profound theological reflection on his ministry as an apostle of the new covenant (3:1–6:10). Since the Lectionary will make use of four more texts from this section (4:6-11; 4:13–5:1; 5:6-10; 5:14-17), preachers will do well to read and reflect on this material which has implications for their ministry as well.

Paul's discussion about his ministry was occasioned by his recent dealings with the Corinthians who had already questioned his apostolic integrity because he failed to visit them as he had promised. In the meantime other Christian missionaries had come to Corinth with letters recommending them to the Corinthian community. Who they were, we do not know. Some commentators argue that they were Jewish Christians with a strong attachment to the Mosaic covenant, as well as to Christ. Enamored of these newcomers, some of the Corinthians criticized Paul's ministry all the more. Thus it was necessary for him to say something in defense of his ministry.

Paul's first response is that he has no need for letters of recommendation to, or from, the Corinthians, as do others, because they themselves are his letter of recommendation. That is to say, the work that he has done as a minister of Christ speaks for itself. Whereas others have come to Corinth with letters written in ink, Paul's letter is the Corinthian community, formed by the Spirit of the living God. This makes Paul the minister of a new covenant that derives its power from the Spirit of God rather than from the tablets of the Mosaic Law, upon which Paul's rivals still rely.

The reference to a new covenant leads to a comparison between the ministry of the new covenant, of which Paul is a minister, and the ministry of the old covenant, which Moses administered (3:7-18). Although the Lectionary does not draw on this comparison, it will be helpful to say something about it.

Briefly put, Paul argues that even though the ministry of the Mosaic covenant was glorious, its glory paled in comparison to the glory of the new covenant of which Paul is a minister. Thus, whenever Moses spoke with God, his face became radiant with the reflected glory of God. That glory, however, was destined to end. Consequently, whenever Moses spoke to the people, he veiled his face, an indication to Paul that the ministry of the old covenant was ending. As a minister of the new covenant, Paul says that he is bolder than Moses since his gospel reveals Christ, the image of God and the final revelation of God's enduring glory. Those who believe in the gospel of the new covenant, therefore, are transformed from glory to glory as they look upon the face of Christ, the image of God.

This section is almost too rich to preach. Preachers, however, might reflect on one of the two themes that occur in this text. First, the believing community is a creation of Christ or, as Paul says, a letter of Christ. This means that the Church does not establish itself, nor do people decide to become the Church. The Church is a creation of God effected by the power of God's Spirit.

Second, as the creation of Christ, the Church is a manifestation of the new covenant that God has established through the death and resurrection of Christ, the covenant promised in Jeremiah:

> The days are coming, says the Lord, when I will make a new covenant with the house of Israel and the house of Judah. . . . I will place my law within them, and write it upon their hearts; I will be their God, and they shall be my people (Jer 31:31, 33b).

For Paul, the new covenant is marked by the powerful presence of the Spirit which enables believers to know and do God's will in a way that the written code could and did not. Preachers will do well to remind their congregation what it means to belong to the community of the new covenant. Preachers will also want to consider what it means for them to be apostolic ministers of this new covenant.

The Sufferings of an Apostle
Ninth Sunday: 2 Cor 4:6-11

Continuing the theme of glory, Paul notes that the light of God has shone in his heart so that he could bring the knowledge of the glory of God to others. This light first illumined Paul's heart when God called him to be the Apostle to the Gentiles. Consequently, the glory that Paul reveals is none other than God's own glory which shines on the face of Christ.

Having spoken of glory, Paul turns to the sufferings he endures an apostle. In doing so, he counters one of the criticisms the Corinthians directed against him: that he is not a powerful apostle, nor does he measure up to the rival preachers who came to Corinth with letters of recommendation. Instead, he is weak and infirm, overcome by the sufferings of his ministry. Rather than deny this criticism, Paul accepts it. He is not ashamed of his sufferings since they authenticate him as a minister of the new covenant. The Corinthians and their newly arrived visitors do not understand that the glorious ministry of the new covenant is always held in frail and mortal bodies that are dying daily, for the surpassing glory belongs to God and not to the minister. While this may perplex some, it does not disturb Paul who has conformed himself to Christ's sufferings. He is a minister of the new covenant because of his sufferings, not in spite of them. As he is being given up to death each day, the life of Jesus is made manifest in his mortal body.

Although this reading concludes at 4:11, preachers should take into consideration the following verse, "So death is at work in us, but life in you" (4:12). In this statement, Paul affirms that his apostolic sufferings are redemptive. Consequently, whereas the Corinthians criticize him as a suffering apostle, he views his sufferings as redemptive for them.

This portrait of the suffering apostle provides preachers with an opportunity to proclaim the paradox of the gospel: power in weakness, life in death, the surpassing glory of the new covenant which is manifested in preachers who are as fragile as earthen vessels. It is an occasion to discuss the nature of ministry which is rooted in the dying and rising of Christ rather than in the person of the minister. It may even be an opportunity to ask congregations what kind of ministry they encourage: the ministry of the new covenant as exemplified by Paul or a ministry that depends on human praise.

Inner Renewal
Tenth Sunday: 2 Cor 4:13–5:1

This reading continues Paul's description of the sufferings he endures as a minister of the new covenant. It begins with an affirmation of his confidence that is similar to the confidence of the Psalmist, "I believed, therefore I spoke" (4:13). More specifically,

Paul believes in the God who raises the dead, confident that if God raised Jesus from the dead, God will also raise those who believe in him.

This confidence in the God who raises the dead leads to the second part of the reading in which Paul explains why the sufferings he endures do not discourage him. He is profoundly aware that these sufferings are transforming him. Thus, while the outer self, which everyone can see, is wasting away, the inner self, which cannot be seen, is being transformed daily.

At this point, Paul introduces the theme of glory again, but now in relation to the daily sufferings of his apostolate. His faith in the God who raises the dead convinces him that his sufferings are integral to final participation in God's glory. As he suffers each day for the sake of the gospel, his inner self, which he cannot see, is being transformed as he prepares to share in Christ's resurrection.

This text provides preachers with an occasion to address the question of suffering. In doing so they should remember that Paul is speaking about sufferings that come to him as he preaches the gospel. He does not glorify suffering for its own sake, nor does he encourage others to seek suffering. Rather, he provides an explanation for the sufferings that beset him as a minister of the gospel: they are part of a process of inner transformation that leads to glory. Preachers may wish to develop a similar theme. Christians do not seek suffering for its own sake, but they believe that it is transformative if endured in and for Christ.

By Faith and Not by Sight
Eleventh Sunday: 2 Cor 5:6-10

This text belongs to a larger unit that includes 5:1-10 which, in turn, is closely related to last week's reading. Still reflecting on the sufferings he endures as a minister of the new covenant, Paul provides a further reason for his confidence: even if his sufferings result in death and his body is destroyed, God will provide him with a heavenly body, the resurrection body. For Paul's discussion of this, preachers should consult 2 Cor 5:1-5, the unit that immediately precedes this reading.

In light of what he has said in 2 Cor 5:1-5 about the resurrection body he hopes to attain, in this week's reading Paul speaks of being "at home in the body" and going "home to the Lord." The first expression refers to Paul's present bodily state, characterized by apostolic suffering, while the second alludes to the resurrection life he will enjoy when his body will be immortal and incorruptible, transformed by God's glory, and no longer liable to pain, suffering, and death.

Although he longs to be with the Lord, this hope allows Paul to remain confident during this time of apostolic suffering. Thus he says that he walks by faith and not by sight. Preachers should relate this expression to what Paul said in last week's reading about the inner and outer self. Whereas one can see the outer self which is wasting away, one must believe that God is transforming the inner self in preparation for the resurrection body.

The material of this reading is not easy to deal with, even if the congregation were to hear the entire passage. It is one of those passages that needs to be taught in an adult education session. Nevertheless, preachers can profitably focus on the theme of walking by faith rather than by sight. For, while most people want to see in order to believe, the gospel proclaims that we must believe in order to see. Thus, whereas the Corinthians looked at Paul and could not see beyond his sufferings, Paul believed in what he could not see: that his inner self was being transformed by these sufferings. When Christians walk by faith, they see what others cannot.

A Ministry of Reconciliation
Twelfth Sunday: 2 Cor 5:14-17

Thus far Paul has explained his ministry in terms of glory and suffering. On the one hand, as a minister of the new covenant, his gospel discloses the glory of God reflected on the face of Christ who is the image of God (3:1–4:6). On the other, his ministry is marked by suffering and pain. What is seen, Paul's outer self, is dying daily; but his inner self, which is not seen, is being transformed daily. Having made these two points, Paul turns to a third. The ministry of the new covenant is a ministry of reconciliation rooted in the death of Christ.

The theme of reconciliation is developed in 5:11-21, especially in vv. 17-21. However, since the Lectionary reading only draws upon vv. 14-17, preachers will need to reflect on the entire unit if they hope to make sense of this reading.

The unit begins with Paul defending himself against accusations that he commends himself too much. He insists that he is not so much trying to commend himself to the Corinthians as he is providing them with an opportunity to boast in his ministry when confronted by those who boast in their ministry (see 5:11-13). Everything, then, is for the sake of the Corinthians. It is at this point (5:14) that the Lectionary reading begins with Paul explaining why he acts as he does: the love of Christ impels him.

The love of Christ is not so much Paul's love for Christ as Christ's love for him. The conviction that Christ died for all has transformed Paul's life, for he now realizes that he ought to live no longer for himself but for Christ who died and rose for the sake of all.

Christ's love for all, manifested in his death on the cross, radically altered how Paul understood Christ. Whereas he once viewed him from a merely human point of view ("according to the flesh"), persecuting his followers as fanatics and apostates, he now understands that the crucified Messiah was none other than the Son of God who gave his life for the sake of all. This leads Paul to the remarkable conclusion that those who are in Christ "are a new creation." They are the new humanity inaugurated by the new Adam.

The Lectionary reading concludes at this point. The following verses (5:18-21), however, develop the theme of the new creation in terms of reconciliation. Believers are a new creation because God was reconciling the world to himself through Christ, and Paul is God's ambassador of reconciliation, calling all who will listen to be reconciled to God. Thus the ministry of the new covenant is a ministry of reconciliation.

God, of course, does not need to be reconciled to humanity. Humanity, however, is in profound need of a reconciliation which it cannot effect on its own behalf. That is why God reconciled the world to himself through Christ, and it is why Paul calls on humanity to be reconciled to God through faith in Jesus Christ.

Today's world is in profound need of healing and reconciliation, and this is a good place for preachers who have been entrusted with a ministry of reconciliation to begin their reflection on this text. This reconciliation has two dimensions: one horizontal (reconciliation between human beings), the other vertical (reconciliation between humanity and God). While the contemporary world focuses on the former, the gospel reminds us that the ground of all reconciliation is what God has done in Christ. Because God has reconciled humanity to himself, making it a new creation, human beings can and should reconcile themselves to each other.

The Poverty of Christ
Thirteenth Sunday: 2 Cor 8:7, 9, 13-15

In the first seven chapters of 2 Corinthians, Paul has reflected on his apostolic ministry. After discussing his ministry in terms of the new covenant, suffering, and reconciliation, he calls the community to be reconciled with him (see 7:2-4, a section of the letter that the Lectionary does not include).

Having defended his ministry and called the community to reconciliation, in chapters 8–9 Paul turns to the question of the collection for the poor of Jerusalem. A year earlier, the Corinthians made a start in collecting alms for the poor of Jerusalem, but they did not complete their offering because of their conflict with Paul. Now that this conflict has been resolved, Paul encourages the community to complete the work it began so that their gift will be ready when he arrives.

Although a discussion about this collection may seem a rather mundane matter, it was not so for Paul. For Paul, the collection signified the communion between Jewish and Gentile believers, a way for Gentile believers to express their gratitude to the people of Israel from whom the Messiah came. If the church of Jerusalem accepted this gift, it would be an acknowledgement of Paul's ministry among the Gentiles. Thus, he hoped that this collection would solidify Jewish and Gentile relations.

What is so remarkable about this reading is the manner in which Paul motivates the Corinthians to complete what they have begun. Their generosity should be rooted in the generosity of Jesus Christ who, though he was rich, became poor for their sake, so that through his poverty they might become rich. This remarkable statement (8:9) alludes to Christ's preexistence and recalls the Philippian hymn (Phil 2:6-11) which describes how the preexistent one did not insist on the privilege of divinity but humbled himself to the point of dying a slave's death on the cross.

The example of Christ, then, becomes a model for the Corinthians to follow as they collect alms for the poor of Jerusalem. The abundance they enjoy at the present time should supply the needs of those who are less fortunate. Conversely, if the Corinthians find themselves in dire circumstances, Paul anticipates that the believers at Jerusalem will assist them. Thus, there will be equality among the churches.

This text is a model of Paul's pastoral method. No problem is too ordinary. Accordingly, he resolves all problems in light of the gospel. Preachers might explain this background in order to show their congregations how the gospel sheds light on seemingly secular matters. Or, they might focus on the example of Christ who became poor so that humanity might become rich. In doing so, they will challenge their congregations to rethink in light of the gospel what it means to be poor and rich. Riches that are not shared with those in need lead to inner poverty, whereas emptying oneself for the sake of others leads to authentic wealth.

Power in Weakness
Fourteenth Sunday: 2 Cor 12:7-10

Chapters 10–13 form the third section of 2 Corinthians, and it is somewhat disappointing that the Lectionary does not make greater use of them. Their background can be summarized in this way.

Having called the community to reconciliation in chapters 1–7 and encouraged it to complete the collection in chapters 8–9, in chapters 10–13 Paul deals with the outsiders who have caused him so much difficulty. By coming to Corinth they have intruded into his mission field. More importantly, they have extolled themselves at his expense, accusing him of writing strong letters but being a rather poor orator. As they see it, Paul has taken advantage of the community.

Paul is aware of these accusations and seems to know a great deal about these outsiders whom he sarcastically calls "super-apostles." From his point of view, they boast too much in their power and strength, and they do not appreciate the role of suffering and weakness in the apostolic life. Therefore, Paul minces no words; they are false apostles and ministers of Satan who masquerade as apostles of Christ (11:13).

Paul, however, must deal with them, even though he would prefer to avoid boasting about himself. Consequently, he takes a rather interesting tack in the final chapters of this letter. In contrast to the super-apostles who boast in their Jewish pedigree, their skill as orators, and their visionary experiences, Paul boasts in his sufferings and weakness.

The text for this week is part of a larger unit in which Paul engages in foolish boasting (11:16–12:10). Therefore, preachers should read the entire text carefully. The speech begins with Paul boasting about his Jewish pedigree but quickly turns to the sufferings and humiliations that he has endured as an apostle of Christ. Thus, in chapter 12, Paul recounts a visionary experience in which he was taken into heaven, but he concludes by saying that he was given a thorn in the flesh lest he become proud.

Paul's strategy through these chapters is clear: the paradoxical message of the gospel is that God reveals his power in weakness, just as he did on the cross. Thus, Paul concludes that when he is strong then he is weak. The super-apostles have not yet learned the paradox of the cross, and until they do, they cannot be genuine ministers of Christ.

Preachers have a marvelous opportunity to deal with the paradoxical message of the cross. To do so they must read these chapters and reflect on the ways in which Paul boasts in his suffering and weakness rather than in power and strength. They will do well to deal with Paul's insight that when he is weak, then he is strong, for power is made perfect in weakness. The key to comprehending this paradox is the cross; for, when believers relinquish their power and strength, as Christ did on the cross, God fills them with resurrection life.

Strategy: Theological Themes

Those who preach from 2 Corinthians have an opportunity to develop a number of theological themes related to ministry and Christology. I summarize these under two headings.

Christological themes. In 2 Corinthians, Paul makes use of a number of christological themes. For example, in defending his integrity, he reminds the Corinthians of the integrity of Christ who fulfilled all of God's promises by rendering perfect obedience to God (1:19-20). In describing himself as the minister of a new covenant, Paul presents Christ as the image of God on whose face the glory of God is perfectly reflected (3:12–4:6). In calling the Corinthians to reconciliation, he portrays Christ as the one through whom God reconciled the world to himself, the one who died for all (5:11-21). When encouraging the Corinthians to complete the collection for the poor, he reminds them of the Son of God who, though he was rich, became poor so that they might become rich (8:9). Finally, when comparing himself with the super-apostles, Paul refers to the power of Christ which manifests itself in the weakness of Paul's ministry (12:9).

In preaching from 2 Corinthians, it is important to remember that Paul's primary concern is what God has done through Christ. God is the primary actor in the drama of salvation, and Christ is the agent through whom God accomplishes his purposes. Thus, Christ fulfills God's promise, reflects God's glory and, through him, God reconciled the world to himself.

At the present time there is a great deal of interest in the person of the historical Jesus, and rightly so, since Christianity is rooted in the life of an historical person. The role of the preacher is to remind the congregation of what God has done in this historical person and the paradoxical nature of the gospel in which transcendent power manifests itself through human weakness.

Ministerial Themes. 2 Corinthians provides readers with Paul's most profound meditation on the nature of apostolic ministry. It is a ministry of the new covenant whose purpose is to reveal the glory of God that shines on the face of Christ and call people to reconciliation. Ministers of the new covenant are ambassadors for Christ (5:20). And like ambassadors, they do not represent themselves but another.

Ministers of the new covenant, however, carry out their ministry amidst the sufferings and trials of daily life. Those who judge the ministers of the new covenant on the basis of appearances do not comprehend the paradoxical relationship between suffering and glory. They do not understand that the ministers of the new covenant are being transformed through their sufferings.

This paradoxical relationship between suffering and glory should be a major theme for those who preach from 2 Corinthians. If it is, it will allow preachers to discuss the paradoxical nature of the Christian life. On the one hand, believers are being transformed from glory to glory as they gaze upon the glory of God reflected on the face of Christ. Believers are bound for glory! The journey is not complete, however, and in the time between now and then, believers must endure suffering, weakness, and pain. Their outer self does not yet correspond to their inner self.

Ephesians

Strategy: Understanding the Context

The Lectionary draws upon Paul's Letter to the Ephesians for seven weeks during Year B. Although the readings are taken from every chapter of the letter except chapters 3 and 6, they tend to focus on the second part of the letter in which Paul exhorts his readers to live a moral life.

The historical context. Ephesians presents a number of historical and critical problems that need not be discussed from the pulpit, but it is helpful for those who preach from this letter to be aware of them.

The two most important problems concern the questions of authorship and audience. While the letter purports to be from Paul to the Ephesians, its literary style and theological content have led many to question its Pauline authorship. And, while some manuscripts name the Ephesians as the recipients of the letter, others do not. Consequently, the letter is usually categorized as one of the "deutero-Pauline" letters: letters that others wrote in Paul's name. Among the deutero-Pauline letters are

Colossians, a writing similar in style and theology to Ephesians, 2 Thessalonians, 1 and 2 Timothy, and Titus.

If contemporary scholars are correct, Ephesians was written by someone intimately acquainted with Paul's thought, and it was sent as a circular letter to a number of Gentile congregations in Asia Minor. Its purpose was two-fold: (1) to remind these Gentile congregations of the divine election that made them members of the commonwealth of Israel, and (2) to exhort them to live a moral life which corresponds to their election.

Knowledge that Ephesians may have been written by someone other than Paul can be helpful to preachers because it prepares them for the subtle shifts of theology that occur in this letter when compared with the Pauline correspondence discussed thus far. Among these shifts I note the author's emphasis on the Church universal as compared with Paul's focus on the local congregation. The author of Ephesians views the Church as a cosmic reality which embodies a new humanity whose head is Christ.

Having made the point that Ephesians may not have been written by Paul, I wish to stress that the proper setting for discussing such historical questions is an adult education session rather than the homily since the homily does not provide an opportunity for people to ask questions. In preaching Ephesians, or any deutero-Pauline letter, preachers should refer to the author of these letters as Paul, for this is the manner in which the canon identifies them. More importantly, Paul's followers were faithful to his theological vision.

The literary context. Ephesians can be divided into two parts. In the first (1:1–3:21), Paul celebrates the divine election of his Gentile converts. Blessing God and giving thanks in chapter 1 for all that has been accomplished in Christ, in chapter 2 he reminds the Ephesians of their former status apart from Christ. At that time, they lived in sin and were alienated from the people of Israel. But now, God has reconciled Gentile and Jew in Christ, making them the beginning of a new humanity. Paul, who writes this letter from prison, has been entrusted with this mystery: "that the Gentiles are coheirs, members of the same body, and copartners in the promise in Christ Jesus through the gospel" (3:6). Profoundly humbled that the mystery of Gentile and Jew has been entrusted to him, he concludes the first part of Ephesians with a prayer of gratitude (3:14-21).

Having reminded the Ephesians of their election and the mystery that has been entrusted to him, Paul devotes chapters 4–6 to moral exhortation. Because the Ephesians have been chosen and elected, they should no longer live as the Gentiles do, for they belong to a new humanity. Their warfare is with spiritual powers, and they will do well to become imitators of God (5:1).

Ephesians provides a marvelous example of how Paul's moral exhortation rests on God's redemptive work in Christ. Instead of merely exhorting believers to live a moral life, Paul reminds them of what God has accomplished for them in Christ. In Christ, God elected, chose, and redeemed them, therefore, they ought to live a moral life corresponding to the gospel. Put another way, the imperative to live a moral life rests on the indicative of salvation.

Those who preach from Ephesians should note that the first two readings (1:3-14; 2:13-18) come from the first part of the letter which celebrates God's redemptive work, whereas the remaining texts (4:1-6; 4:17, 20-24; 4:30–5:2; 5:15-20; 5:21-32) are drawn from the letter's moral exhortation. To preach effectively from Paul's moral exhortation, preachers must remember what Paul has said about salvation and election in the first part of the letter. And, as they preach from the first part of the letter, they will do well to reflect on the implications of this material for the moral exhortation that will follow.

Strategy: The Text in Its Context

God's Plan in Christ
Fifteenth Sunday: Eph 1:3-14

This magnificent blessing, which stands at the beginning of Ephesians, is foundational for what Paul will say in the rest of the letter. Marveling at the magnificent plan of God revealed in Christ, the apostle praises the God and Father of Jesus Christ.

Although the motivation for this praise is multifaceted, it is always centered on God's work in Christ. Thus, God has blessed believers with every spiritual blessing *in Christ*, chosen them *in Christ* before the foundation of the world, and destined them for adoption *through Jesus Christ. In Christ*, believers have redemption by his blood, and now, in the fullness of time, God has set forth his plan to restore all things *in Christ*. The purpose of existence is to praise God for his glory. Believers have already been sealed with the Holy Spirit, the first installment of the inheritance that will be theirs.

Although there are a multiplicity of themes in this benediction, it continually returns to the plan of God revealed in Christ. The life, death, and resurrection of Christ have disclosed something hidden for ages but now revealed. More specifically, God has disclosed his purpose to restore all things in Christ.

What Paul says in this benediction undergirds the moral exhortation in the second part of the letter. For, if God has chosen and elected the Ephesians in Christ, they can no longer live as they formerly did. The plan of God revealed in Christ summons them to praise God for all that has been done in Christ. It calls them to live lives that are holy and blameless.

For many people, the world appears to be a chaotic place with no rhyme or reason. The opening benediction of Ephesians, however, provides preachers with an opportunity to present an alternative vision of the world, one in which God's plan is to restore all things in Christ. This vision is not evident to everybody, and preachers should be aware of this. The restoration of all things in Christ is the mystery that God has revealed and Paul must explain. Just as Paul found it necessary to explain this mystery to the Ephesians, so preachers will find it necessary to remind their congregations of God's plan and their role in it.

Humanity Reconciled and Renewed
Sixteenth Sunday: Eph 2:13-18

In this text Paul states his thesis that Christ has reconciled Gentile and Jew in himself, thereby creating one new person. This thesis, however, is embedded in a broader literary context.

The wider context begins in chapter 2, where Paul reminds the Ephesians of their former way of life. At one time they were dead because of their trespasses and sins (2:1). Moreover, because they were uncircumcised, they were alienated from the commonwealth of Israel and had no share in the covenants and promises of God's people (2:11-12). God who is rich in mercy and love, however, gave them life with Christ, so that they have been saved by grace (2:5). In Christ, God created the Gentiles anew.

Having described the woeful condition of his readers apart from Christ, Paul next explains their new status in Christ. First Christ broke down the dividing wall that separated them from Israel so that he might reconcile Gentile and Jew in his body, thereby creating one new person. The dividing wall was the Mosaic Law that functioned as a social barrier between Gentiles and Jews, forbidding Jews to share table fellowship with Gentiles who did not observe the ritual prescriptions of the Law. In dying on the cross, Christ put an end to the Mosaic Law making Gentiles and Jews one in his body.

This union of Gentiles and Jews in Christ is the mystery that has been revealed by the Spirit to the apostles and prophets of the Church: "that the Gentiles are coheirs, members of the same body, and copartners in the promise in Christ Jesus through the gospel" (3:6). This body is the body of Christ, the Church, of which Christ is the head (see 1:22-23).

Paul's thesis, that Christ has brought Gentile and Jewish believers together is another aspect of his teaching on justification by faith apart from the Law. In effect, Paul is explaining the social dimension of his teaching on justification by grace through faith. He is saying that God reconciles individuals by reconciling communities of peoples to himself.

This text is an opportunity to discuss the scope of God's reconciling work in Christ which envisions the unity of all people in Christ. Enmity among people is contrary to God's purpose. It is all the more perfidious when it occurs within the Church, for God intends the Church to be the body of Christ in which all enmity is overcome. The catholicity of the Church is its ability to embrace people of diverse racial and ethnic backgrounds so that they can become one new person in Christ.

A Life Worthy of One's Call
Seventeenth Sunday: Eph 4:1-6

This text marks the beginning of Paul's moral exhortation, the second part of the letter. This extended exhortation can be divided into four sections. First, there is an initial exhortation to maintain the unity of the Spirit so that the Church will grow in love into its head, who is Christ (4:1-16). Second, there are three brief exhortations not to live morally dissolute lives as the Gentiles do (4:17-24; 4:25–5:2; 5:3-14). Third, there is an exhortation concerned with the internal life of the Church, especially the Christian household (5:15–6:9). Finally, there is an exhortation to take up the armor of God since the moral life involves a struggle against spiritual powers (6:10-20).

The text for this week is part of a larger unit (4:1-16), the first of four exhortations. It begins by reminding readers that Paul is imprisoned, presumably for the sake of the gospel. His own life serves as an example to others and provides him with the moral authority to call them to lead a life worthy of their calling.

To explain what he means, Paul provides his readers with a list of virtues (humility, gentleness, patience, love) that will assist them in maintaining the unity of the Spirit. Just as there is one body, one Spirit, one Lord, one faith, one baptism, and one God and Father, there should be unity of mind and heart within the Church. Paul's vision of the Church is that of a body in which every part works properly and promotes the growth of the whole body in love (4:16).

If last week's reading provided an opportunity to speak about the catholicity of the Church, this week's offers an occasion to discuss its unity. That unity is rooted in one Lord, one faith, one baptism. But if it is to be effective in the lives of believers, their lives must correspond with the faith they profess in Christ. Thus faith and ethics are related. What believers do ought to reflect what they believe, and what they believe should determine what they do.

Putting away the Old Self
Eighteenth Sunday: Eph 4:17, 20-24

This is the first of three brief exhortations (4:17-24; 4:24–5:2; 5:3-14) in which Paul exhorts the Ephesians not to live as the Gentiles do. It is remarkable for the manner in which it begins, "you must no longer live as the Gentiles do" (4:17), since the recipients of the letter were Gentiles! However, now that they have been incorporated into the Church, they are no longer Gentiles, from Paul's point of view. Rather, in the Church they form the new person that is emerging with Christ as its head. Neither Gentile nor Jew, they form a new person that embraces both.

Paul characterizes their former way of life as the old self that was corrupted and deluded by desire and lust. In contrast to the old self stands the new self created in truth, righteousness, and holiness. The language that Paul employs here is reminiscent of the Adam Christ comparison he drew in Romans 5. Either one stands in solidarity with Adam, the progenitor of the old humanity, or with Christ, the progenitor of the new humanity.

Paul is a realist. Although he identifies the recipients of this letter as a people chosen and elected in Christ, he is keenly aware that they have not yet set aside their former way of life. Too many are straddling the fence between the new and the old self, between loyalty to Adam and loyalty to Christ. The purpose of this initial exhortation, then, is to remind them of who they are, so that they will leave behind what they were.

The moral exhortation of Ephesians, and this exhortation in particular, provides an excellent example of Paul's pastoral theology. Instead of simply telling people what they ought to do, he reminds his congregations who they are, confident that moral action flows from moral identity. Contemporary preachers ought to follow a similar model as they exhort their congregations to live holy and righteous lives. Instead of telling people what to do, preachers would do well to remind their congregations of their dignity in Christ. Those who know who they are in Christ will, by God's grace, live accordingly.

Be Imitators of God
Nineteenth Sunday: Eph 4:30–5:2

This text is the second of three exhortations (4:17-24; 4:25–5:2; 5:3-14) which summons the Ephesians to live in a way that corresponds with the gospel they have embraced. Preachers will want to review the whole unit, especially its first verse which provides another rationale for living the moral life: "Therefore, putting away falsehood, speak the truth, each one to his neighbor, for we are members one of another" (4:25). At the outset of this exhortation Paul establishes an ecclesial ethic. Members of the Church have a moral responsibility to each other because they are members of the body of Christ. They belong to each other because they belong to Christ.

After explaining the kind of behavior that is foreign to the members of Christ's body (4:26-29), Paul exhorts his audience not to grieve the Holy Spirit of God with which they were sealed in anticipation of their redemption. This reference to the Spirit recalls Paul's earlier statement, in the great benediction, that the Ephesians "were sealed with the promised holy Spirit, which is the first installment of our inheritance toward redemption as God's possession, to the praise of his glory" (Eph 1:13-14).

Two points are important here. First, the gift of the Spirit is the pledge or guarantee of an inheritance yet to be obtained, final redemption. The fact that the Ephesians have been sealed with God's Spirit serves as their assurance or guarantee that they will receive this inheritance. Second, because the Spirit identifies believers as those destined for final redemption, immoral conduct contradicts who they are. It grieves God's Holy Spirit when those destined for redemption live according to the old self.

To insure that believers do not grieve God's Spirit, Paul exhorts them to be imitators of God. The expression is rather unusual. Paul normally exhorts his converts to imitate him since he has conformed himself to the crucified Christ. The language he uses here, however, is rooted in the Old Testament, especially the exhortation of Lev 19:2, "Speak to the whole Israelite community and tell them: Be holy, for I, the LORD, your God, am holy." Similar language is found in the Matthean version of

Jesus' great Sermon in which Jesus exhorts his disciples to be perfect as their heavenly Father is perfect (Matt 5:48), and in the Lucan version which calls upon disciples to be merciful as their heavenly Father is merciful (Luke 6:36).

Paul explains what it means to imitate God by pointing to the example of Christ who loved us and gave himself for us (5:2). True imitation of God is sacrificial love, as exemplified by Christ's death upon the cross. This is the ecclesial ethic to which Paul summons the Church.

Those who preach from Ephesians will find these readings repetitious only if they focus on what Paul tells his audience *not* to do. The theological richness of these readings, however, is found in the religious motivation they provide for believers to live a moral life. Believers live moral lives because they are the new humanity whose head is Christ. They are members of each other. They have been sealed by the Holy Spirit of God. Their vocation is to be imitators of God as was Christ. There is a rich treasure in these texts if one focuses on these motivating factors, reminding congregations that the Christian moral life flows from being in Christ.

The Proper Use of Time
Twentieth Sunday: Eph 5:15-20

The readings for the next two weeks are taken from the third part of Paul's moral exhortation (5:15–6:9), in which the Apostle deals with the internal life of the community, especially the Christian household. The text for this week is the beginning of that exhortation.

Immediately preceding this reading, Paul provides a brief moral exhortation that the Sunday Lectionary does not include (5:3-14). Preachers should reflect on it, however, since it serves as the immediate context for this text and offers another reason for living the moral life: "For you were once darkness, but now you are light in the Lord. Live as children of light" (5:8).

When the Ephesians were in darkness, they lived foolishly. Now that they have become children of the light, they must live as people who are wise. Those who are wise understand the importance of the time at their disposal, and they make the most of it by living according to God's will. Whereas the foolish become intoxicated with life's immediate pleasures, the wise are intoxicated with God's Spirit, the guarantee of their redemption. It is that Spirit which enables them to praise God with psalms, hymns, and spiritual songs.

As busy as people are, most have more time at their disposal than they realize. Therefore, it is not unusual for people to seek the advice of time consultants to determine the best use of time. Paul's letter to the Ephesians also has something to say about the use of time, but it is not the practical advice most people expect. It establishes two sets of contrasts: being foolish and being wise; being intoxicated with life's pleasures and being intoxicated with God's Spirit. In light of these contrasts, it calls on believers to make the best use of their time by living in accordance with God's will.

Mutual Subordination
Twenty-first Sunday: Eph 5:21-32

This text is part of a larger household code that includes the relationship between children and parents, slaves and masters (see 5:21–6:9). Such codes were common in the Greco-Roman world. They were also important for the ordering of society which functions best when everyone knows his or her role.

Ephesians, Colossians, and 1 Peter employ household codes to instruct converts in the moral life. In adopting the basic form and structure of these codes, however, they also introduce new elements in light of the gospel. Thus, these codes originally provided believers with a structured way of living the gospel in light of their time and culture.

The basic structure of the code in Ephesians deals with the relationships between wives and husbands (5:21-33), children and parents (6:1-4), and slaves and masters (6:5-9). The code reflects the cultural assumptions of the day that wives should be subordinate to their husbands, children to their parents, and slaves to their masters. Thus, in each instance, the code begins with the obligations of the weaker party (wives, children, slaves) to the dominant party (husbands, parents, masters).

While the Ephesians code is bound to the cultural assumptions of its day (how could it not be?), preachers should not dismiss it out of hand, for it makes a number of significant advances when compared to the secular household codes of its day. Among the most important are the gospel obligations of the more dominant party toward the subordinate. Thus husbands are to love their wives *as* Christ loved his Church, when he handed himself over for the sake of the Church. Fathers are not to provoke their children but train them in the instruction of the Lord, and masters must remember that they have a master in heaven.

These codes pose a problem for contemporary believers who live in a culture that has abolished slavery and no longer views women as subordinate to men. Thus many preachers find themselves faced with a dilemma: to ignore the text, giving the impression that the Word of God has failed, or to preach from a text which puzzles and embarrasses them. To me, it seems more prudent to deal with the text rather than ignore it. But how? I offer two strategies.

First, preachers must say something about the culture that gave birth to these codes. That culture assumed the subordination of certain members of society to others. In this regard, it would be helpful to indicate that every culture has its hidden assumptions that will become apparent in time. It would be interesting, for example, to know the hidden assumptions of our culture that will seem strange to our descendants fifty or a hundred years from now.

Second, preachers need to focus on the positive aspects of the text: the comparison of marriage to the covenant relationship between Christ and the Church, the self-sacrificing love of husbands for their wives which should mirror Christ's love for the Church. Most importantly, preachers will want to draw attention to the opening verse: "Be subordinate to one another out of reverence for Christ" (5:21). By beginning the reading with this text, the Lectionary suggests that the deepest meaning of the household code is mutual-subordination rather than the dominance of one partner over the other. Husbands and wives, then, will subordinate themselves to each other as each imitates the self-sacrificing love of Christ for the Church.

Strategy: Theological Themes

Those who preach from Ephesians will have an opportunity to discuss the moral life of believers since the majority of the Lectionary readings come from the letter's moral exhortation. However, since Ephesians grounds this moral exhortation in the good news of the gospel, preachers must be careful to do the same. The best way to exhort people is to remind them of what God has done for them in Christ.

The Plan of God. For Ephesians, nothing has happened by chance. Everything is part of God's plan. Believers were chosen in Christ before the foundation of the world to be holy and blameless (1:4). The moral life, then, is the grateful response of believers to their election in Christ. Although they were in darkness once, now they dwell in light and understand the plan of God. Because they understand the plan of God in Christ, they must live accordingly.

The Mystery of the Church. Integral to the plan of God is the Church, the body of Christ. The Church is the beginning of a new humanity that unites Gentile and Jew in the body of Christ. Thus, it is the manifestation of God's reconciling work in the world. Because the Church is so central to the plan of God, there is an ecclesial dimension to the moral life of believers. They live the moral life within the Church, the body of Christ. Their moral life is an attempt to manifest what they are: the body of Christ, the Church.

Hebrews

Although Paul did not write the Epistle to the Hebrews, I treat it for the following reasons. First, the early Church, especially in the East, numbered Hebrews among the Pauline letters, as did several ancient manuscripts. It is not surprising then that many Christians still think of Hebrews as a Pauline letter, though it makes no claim to Pauline authorship. Second, Hebrews plays a significant role in the Sunday Lectionary, appearing seven times during Year B and four times during Year C. Third, and most importantly, Hebrews is among the most profoundly theological writings of the New Testament.

Like the Pauline Epistles, Hebrews focuses on the significance of Jesus' death and develops a sophisticated christology that identifies Jesus as the preexistent Son of God. It is not surprising then that many of the Eastern Fathers viewed it as coming from Paul's hand. Hebrews, however, develops a number of themes that distinguish it from the Pauline epistles, the most important of which is the high priesthood of Jesus Christ. Arguing that the cult of the levitical priesthood was incapable of dealing with sin, Hebrews presents Jesus as a high priest according to the order of Melchizedek who dealt with sin, once and for all, when he entered into the heavenly sanctuary at his death. This theme occurs several times in the readings of Year B, and I will develop it further when I discuss those readings.

Hebrews also asserts that since Jesus Christ has dealt with sin once and for all, there is no further need for the levitical priesthood and the temple cult. Thus, whereas Paul argued that there is no need to do the works of the Mosaic Law because Christ has justified sinners by dying on the cross, Hebrews argues that there is no need for the levitical priesthood and its cult since Jesus Christ, a high priest according to the order of Melchizedek, dealt with sin once and for all by entering into the heavenly sanctuary. Put another way, whereas Paul says that Christ did what the Law could not do (effect justification), Hebrews says that Christ did what the levitical cult could not do (deal with sin).

Strategy: Understanding the Context

The historical context. The historical background of Hebrews is as mysterious as its theology is profound. The author, the audience, and the occasion for this work are all matters of dispute. First, though the early Church identified Paul as the author of this writing, its author never identifies himself. Second, although this writing is called the Epistle to the Hebrews, this title comes from a later scribe who may have supposed that the recipients were Jewish since Hebrews deals with matters such as the levitical cult. It is possible, however, that the recipients were Gentiles attracted to the Jewish cult. Finally, since we are not sure who the author or recipients were, it is difficult to identify the occasion for this writing. However, the repeated exhortations not to lose heart and the extended treatment of the high priesthood of Christ suggest that Hebrews addresses a group of believers in danger of losing their original fervor. Therefore, Hebrews reminds them of Christ's high priestly work on their behalf and exhorts them to follow in the steps of Jesus, the pioneer and perfecter of their faith (12:2).

The literary context. Although Hebrews is traditionally called an epistle, it does not begin like other letters of the New Testament. Instead of the typical letter greeting and thanksgiving, it opens with an elegant sentence that announces the theme which its author will develop in the rest of the writing (1:1-4) and then proceeds to discuss the superiority of Jesus to the angels of God (1:5-14). It is not surprising, then, that many view this writing as an extended sermon rather than as a letter or epistle. The anonymous author, however, identifies this writing as a "message of encouragement" (13:22), and that is probably the best way to view it.

Hebrews alternates between a doctrinal exposition that focuses on the superiority of Jesus, the Son of God, a high priest according to the order of Melchizedek, and moral exhortation. While the doctrinal exposition of Hebrews attracts the attention of most because of its highly sophisticated christology, the main purpose of the letter is found in its moral exhortation which uses the doctrinal exposition to encourage the audience to change and alter its behavior.

During Year B, the Lectionary draws from the following texts of Hebrews: 2:9-11; 4:12-13; 4:14-16; 5:1-6; 7:23-28; 9:24-28; 10:11-14, 18. The majority of these texts occur within chapters 5–10, the great central section in which Hebrews develops its high priestly christology for the purpose of exhorting its audience not to lose heart. As preachers deal with these texts, they will have an opportunity to focus on one of the great christological themes of the New Testament, the high priesthood of Jesus Christ. In doing so they should remember that Hebrews develops this theme with a view to exhorting believers to live in a particular way. More specifically, believers must follow Jesus, the pioneer and perfecter of their faith, who was made perfect through suffering. Since one of the primary purposes of preaching is moral exhortation, contemporary preachers will find a model for preaching in Hebrews.

Strategy: The Text in Its Context

Jesus and the Destiny of Humanity
Twenty-seventh Sunday: Heb 2:9-11

This text belongs to a wider context that consists of 1:5–2:18, and it is an excellent example of how Hebrews juxtaposes doctrinal exposition and moral exhortation. In 1:5-14 Hebrews employs a number of scriptural quotations to demonstrate the superiority of Jesus, the Son of God, to the angels of God. Having established Jesus' superiority to the angels, in 2:1-4 Hebrews introduces a brief moral exhortation to encourage its audience to pay greater attention to what it has heard. Finally, in 2:5-18 Hebrews returns to doctrinal exposition. However, whereas the focus of the first moral exhortation was the superiority of Jesus to the angels, Hebrews now considers how, for a brief moment, Jesus was made lower than the angels. Thus the material is structured in the following way.

1:5-14	*Exposition*: The Son of God is superior to the angels.
2:1-4	*Exhortation*: Therefore it is important to pay greater attention to the message that has come from the Son of God.
2:5-18	*Exposition*: Jesus, the Son of God, was made lower than the angels before being crowned with glory and honor.

To make sense of this text, which is only a portion of the second doctrinal exposition, preachers must reflect on the whole of 2:5-18 in which Hebrews argues that God subjected the coming world to humanity, and not to the angels. To make this point, Hebrews quotes Psalm 8, which reflects on the grandeur of humanity:

> Yet you have made them little less than a god,
>   crowned them with glory and honor.
> You have given them rule over the works of your hands,
>   put all things at their feet . . . (6-7).

The point of the psalm is that God destined human beings to rule over creation.

Hebrews, however, is aware that humanity does not yet rule over creation as the psalm envisions. Rather, humanity finds itself in slavery because of its fear of death (Heb 2:15). There is, however, one who has already attained the destiny that the psalm envisions: Jesus, the Son of God. He is already crowned with glory and honor, as will be all who follow in his footsteps.

But Jesus did not attain this glory without suffering. For a little while he, who is greater than the angels (1:5-14), was made lower than the angels so that he might taste death for everyone (2:9). Thus Jesus has become the leader of our salvation, made perfect through the suffering he endured. Although Hebrews never uses the word, it is talking about the incarnation of the Son of God who assumed the human condition so that he could save his brothers and sisters from sin and death.

In making this point, Hebrews introduces a notion that occurs several times in this writing: Jesus was made perfect through suffering. In saying this, Hebrews means that the incarnate Son of God learned something that could not be appropriated apart from the incarnation: the concrete meaning of obedience to the Father in daily life.

Today, humanity stills seeks honor and glory for itself as it tries to subdue God's creation through science, business, technology, and other ways. But despite its best efforts, humanity finds itself frustrated and unable to attain its goal. Those who preach from this text may wish to explain that humanity will never attain its true goal apart from following in the footsteps of Jesus, the leader of salvation. To call him the leader of our salvation is to confess that his destiny is the destiny of humanity. To attain glory and honor, humanity must follow in the steps of Jesus who was perfected through suffering.

Exposed by God's Word
Twenty-eighth Sunday: Heb 4:12-13

This brief text occurs toward the end of an extended moral exhortation that consists of 3:1–4:16. The exhortation begins with a comparison of Jesus and Moses that shows the superiority of Jesus the Son of God to Moses the servant of God, both of whom were faithful to God but in different ways. It then moves to an extended exegesis of Psalm 95, especially the verses that read:

> Oh, that today you would hear his voice:
>   Do not harden your hearts as at Meribah,
>   as on the day of Massah in the desert (7-8).

The point of the exegesis is that whereas Jesus the Son was faithful to God, Israel rebelled. Consequently, Israel never entered into God's Sabbath rest. Warning its readers not to rebel as did the wilderness generation, Hebrews promises its audience that it will enter into God's Sabbath rest if it remains faithful. Drawing from Psalm 95, it exhorts its readers, "Harden not your hearts."

It is at this point that Hebrews concludes its moral exhortation with a brief reflection on the Word of God which it compares to a two-edged sword. Just as a sword cuts, divides, and exposes, so the Word of God lays bare and exposes people to God's view. The Word of God renders judgment, just as Psalm 95 does in exposing the disobedience of the wilderness generation.

It often seems that people no longer fear the Word of God. Words and the production of words have become so common that even believers can forget, or refuse to acknowledge, the power and judgment of God's Word. This was not the case for the author of Hebrews who heard God's Word as a word of judgment as well as a word of salvation. That author knew that to hear the Word was to be put under judgment. For, each time the Word is proclaimed, those who hear it must respond, or they will be judged.

A text such as this provides preachers with an opportunity to reflect on the power of God's Word. While it is possible to hear and ignore the Word, as did the wilderness generation, it is not possible to escape God's judgment. Those who hear the Word of God find themselves exposed before the God of judgment and salvation: a God of judgment for those who rebel, a God of salvation for those who are faithful.

Confidence Based on Faith
Twenty-ninth Sunday: Heb 4:14-16

Thus far, the Lectionary texts have not referred to Jesus as a high priest. Beginning with this reading, the theme of Jesus' high priesthood will be developed over the next five weeks as the Lectionary moves through the great central section of Hebrews (chapters 5–10).

In this central section Hebrews shows that Jesus was qualified to be a high priest (5:1-10), explains what it means to call him a high priest according to the order of Melchizedek (7:1-28), and then discusses this priesthood in light of the new covenant established by Jesus' death (8:1–10:18).

These five chapters represent the christological high point of the letter and are the most systematic exposition of christology in the New Testament. Nevertheless, even in this central section, Hebrews introduces an extended exhortation (5:11–6:20) which indicates how christology undergirds its moral exhortation.

The reading for this week (4:14-16) is a transitional section in which Hebrews moves from exhortation to doctrinal exposition. The manner in which it begins, "Therefore, since we have a great high priest who has passed through the heavens, Jesus, the Son of God, let us hold fast to our confession" (4:14), is a marvelous example of doctrine undergirding moral behavior. Believers can and should maintain their confession because they have a high priest who has passed into the heavenly sanctuary.

Having provided its readers with one doctrinal reason for maintaining their confession, Hebrews offers a second. They can approach the throne of grace, and they will find help in time of need because they have a high priest who can sympathize with their weakness, for he was tested in every way. The high priest who has passed through the heavens is the Son of God who, for a while, became lower than the angels "that he might be a merciful and faithful high priest before God to expiate the sins of the people. Because he himself was tested through what he suffered, he is able to help those who are being tested" (2:17-18).

Hebrews offers contemporary believers a reason for confidence and faith, for it proclaims that Jesus Christ is their high priest who makes intercession for them before the throne of God's grace. Moreover, it affirms that this high priest understands and sympathizes with their weakness because he shared in their human condition. If a priest is meant to mediate between God and humanity, then Jesus eminently fulfills this role. As one who suffered with humanity, he understands the weaknesses of his people. As one who has passed through the heavens, he stands before God's throne where he makes intercession for those in need.

Qualified to Be a High Priest
Thirtieth Sunday: Heb 5:1-6

Although contemporary believers readily think of Jesus as the great high priest who offered himself on the wood of the cross, this was not so obvious to many early Christians since Jesus did not belong to the priestly tribe of Levi. Jesus was a layman, a point that is often forgotten. Consequently, having called Jesus a great high priest who has passed through the heavens (4:14), Hebrews must establish that Jesus was qualified to be a priest. Hebrews does this in 5:1-10, though the Lectionary reading (5:1-6) only presents part of the argument.

In this section (5:1-10), Hebrews sets out three qualifications for a high priest. First, he is chosen from among men. Second, he is able to deal gently with those who have sinned because he himself is weak. Third, he does not assume this office, but God bestows it upon him.

Having set out these qualifications, Hebrews begins with the last and shows how Christ fulfills each. First, God bestowed a high priesthood upon Jesus when he said, "You are my Son; this day I have begotten you" (Ps 2:7 quoted in 5:5), and, "You are a priest forever according to the order of Melchizedek" (Ps 110:4 quoted in 5:6). Second, Jesus is a merciful high priest because he learned obedience from what he suffered. Third, God designated Jesus a high priest according to the order of Melchizedek.

As can be seen from the Lectionary reading, the two psalm texts are central to the argument. The first (Ps 2:7) occurs throughout the New Testament and refers to the day of Jesus' resurrection or exaltation. The second (Ps 110:4) is peculiar to Hebrews which seizes upon the verse, "You are a priest forever according to the order of Melchizedek," a text that the author will explain more fully in chapter 7. For the moment it is sufficient to note that Jesus became a high priest according to the order of Melchizedek on the day of his exaltation or enthronement, after suffering on the cross. His priesthood, therefore, is not so much an office that he exercised on earth as an office he presently exercises as God's exalted Son in the heavenly sanctuary in virtue of his obedient death on the cross.

Those who preach from this text might begin with what is too often forgotten: Jesus was a layman. Although his contemporaries addressed him as Rabbi, and many viewed him as a prophet, no one thought of him as a priest, nor did Jesus claim to be a priest. Indeed, one of the most distinguishing aspects of his life was his conflict with the priesthood of the Jerusalem temple. When Hebrews identifies Jesus as a priest, then, it is not thinking of the levitical priesthood but of a unique priesthood that belongs to Jesus, and which he now exercises in the heavenly sanctuary. Hebrews transcends every traditional category of what it means to be a priest and encourages us do the same.

There is a dwindling number of ordained priests in the Roman Catholic Church today, and this is a genuine concern for Catholics. In addressing this shortage, preachers might reflect on Jesus, the high priest from whom all priests derive their priesthood. While the Church may experience a shortage of ordained ministers, it will never be without its high priest, Jesus Christ, who intercedes on its behalf in the heavenly sanctuary.

The Enduring Priesthood of Jesus Christ
Thirty-first Sunday: Heb 7:23-28

This text comes at the conclusion of chapter 7, in which Hebrews explains what it means to call Jesus a high priest according to the order of Melchizedek. Preachers who wish to understand these verses will do well to reflect on the entire chapter.

In chapter 7, Hebrews discusses the figure of Melchizedek in order to explain the meaning of the verse, "You are a priest forever according to the order of Melchizedek." It notes that Melchizedek was eternal, without genealogy, and that he was greater than Abraham from whom he received tithes. Consequently, when the psalmist speaks of a priesthood according to the order of Melchizedek, he refers to an eternal priest, greater than the levitical priests of the old covenant.

Having explained the eternal nature of the priesthood according to Melchizedek, Hebrews highlights two differences between the priesthood of Levi and the priesthood of Christ. First, the old covenant required many priests because death prevented them from continuing in office. As each generation died, it needed to be replenished by another. Second, and more importantly, the old priesthood offered daily sacrifices that did not deal effectively with sin, but Christ dealt with sin once and for all by a single sacrifice of himself.

Thus, Hebrews says that there is no further need for the priesthood of the old covenant because Jesus' singular sacrifice dealt with sin once and for all. Those who choose to preach from Hebrews might use this occasion to remind their congregations of the unique nature of Jesus' priesthood. That eternal priesthood makes every other priesthood irrelevant *unless* it participates in the priesthood of Jesus Christ. Moreover, it makes every other sacrifice irrelevant *unless* it is a participation in the one sacrifice of Jesus Christ. In a word, Hebrews proclaims that there is one priest and one sacrifice. In assembling for the Eucharist each week, the Christian community, united with its high priest, sacramentally participates in this sacrifice which deals with sin once and for all.

Entrance into the Heavenly Sanctuary
Thirty-second Sunday: Heb 9:24-28

Having explained that the priesthood of Christ is superior to that of the levitical priesthood, in 8:1–10:18 Hebrews compares and contrasts the singular sacrifice that Christ offered with the daily sacrifices the levitical priests offer. Thus, in chapter 8 Hebrews argues that Jesus is the mediator of a better covenant since he has obtained a more excellent ministry (8:6). This better covenant is the new covenant announced in Jer 31:31-34, a text that Hebrews quotes in full. Hebrews sees the fulfillment of this text in Jesus' high priestly sacrifice which effects the forgiveness of sins promised by Jeremiah: "For I will forgive their evil-doing and remember their sins no more" (8:12).

Having introduced the theme of the new covenant and the forgiveness of sins in chapter 8, in chapter 9 Hebrews makes a careful comparison of the old and new cults and the effects of their sacrifices. Hebrews argues that the cult of the old covenant could not effect the forgiveness of sins because it merely offered the bloody sacrifices of irrational animals who could not offer themselves voluntarily in sacrifice. In contrast to them, Christ freely offered himself as a sacrifice for sins by shedding his own blood.

The Lectionary reading for this week develops this argument a step further. Drawing on the imagery of the Day of Atonement (Leviticus 16), when the high priest entered the holy of holies, Hebrews notes that, in contrast to the high priest who entered the earthly sanctuary, Christ entered the heavenly sanctuary with his own blood to atone for sins once and for all. Moreover, whereas the high priest repeated the ritual of atonement every year, there is no need for Christ to repeat his perfect self-offering for the forgiveness of sins. He has entered the true sanctuary, and the sacrifice he offered is sufficient once and for all. Thus, when he returns at the end of the ages, it will not be to take away sins but to bring salvation.

Things are not always what they appear to be. Those who crucified Jesus saw the death of a man they judged to be a criminal. For the author of Hebrews, this gruesome death on the cross was the entrance of the high priest according to the order of Melchizedek into the heavenly sanctuary. For those who executed Jesus, his death served as a warning not to challenge the power of the Roman state. For the author of Hebrews, it was the perfect sacrifice for sins, now and forever.

Everything is a matter of faith and perception. Without faith one sees a criminal, with faith one sees the high priest according to the order of Melchizedek. Without faith one sees a bloody execution, with faith one sees the perfect sacrifice for sins. The task of the preacher is to help the congregation see and perceive what truly happened on the cross.

No Further Offering for Sin
Thirty-third Sunday: Heb 10:11-14, 18

This reading concludes the section in which Hebrews has been comparing the cult and sacrifices of the old and new covenants (8:1–10:18). It also brings to a climax the theme of the new covenant announced by Jeremiah, though the Lectionary reading omits the quotation of Jeremiah found in vv. 16-17. Preachers will do well to read the whole of chapter 10 in order to put the text into context.

At the beginning of chapter 10, Hebrews employs a text from Psalm 40 to show that Christ willingly offered himself as a sacrifice for sins by submitting to God's will:

> "Sacrifice and offering you did not desire,
>   but a body you prepared for me;
> holocausts and sin offerings you took no delight in.
> Then I said, 'As is written of me in the scroll,
> Behold, I come to do your will, O God'" (10:5-7).

From this quotation, Hebrews concludes that what God truly desired was the willing sacrifice of a high priest who offered himself once rather than the animal sacrifices of the old covenant.

Thus the Lectionary reading contrasts the levitical priests who stand day by day offering sacrifices that cannot take away sins with Christ, the high priest, who sits at the right hand of God because his one sacrifice has taken away sins once and for all. At this point, Hebrews repeats the quotation from Jeremiah which the Lectionary does not include, to make the point, "Their sins and their evildoing I will remember no more" (10:17), and it concludes, "Where there is forgiveness of these, there is no longer offering for sin" (10:18).

Although Hebrews makes this powerful statement, even believers can forget that there is no further offering for sin. Because Christ, a high priest according to the order of Melchizedek, has offered himself in sacrifice to God, there is nothing that can or needs to be added to this sacrifice.

Those who preach from this text should reinforce what is often forgotten, even though it is at the heart of the gospel: sins have been forgiven. In an historical event that occurred two thousand years ago, God touched the future as well as the past. Though human beings have, and will continue to sin, their sins have been forgiven. This, of course, is not a license to sin, as if moral behavior no longer matters. To the contrary, the forgiveness of sins is the ground for this moral exhortation and a moral life. Since God has forgiven sins in Christ, believers ought to live moral lives. Thus, immediately after this reading, Hebrews exhorts its audience to a moral life and warns what will happen to those who do not live accordingly (10:19-39; also see, 5:11–6:8).

Strategy: Theological Themes

Hebrews is the most puzzling writing of the New Testament. On the one hand, it appears to be the most cultic writing of the New Testament, the foundation for a theology of cultic worship and priesthood. On the other, it sweeps away all need for priesthood and worship with its affirmation that there is only one priest, Jesus Christ.

To make sense of this paradox, it is helpful to recall that the early Church separated itself from the traditional cult and worship of Israel within a very short period of time. It no longer made use of the levitical priesthood, and it did not experience the temple cult with its daily sacrifices for sins. Moreover, as Christianity moved into Asia Minor and Greece, it quickly became a Gentile phenomenon. The end result was that the first Christians did not have their own temples or places of worship. Nor did they have priests who offered sacrifices for them. The surrounding world perceived this tiny sect of Christians as atheistic; for it had no temple or priests of its own. Christians did not worship in a temple, nor did they offer sacrifices to God.

This situation of being without temple, sacrifice, and priests must have been a cause of concern for many early Christians, and there may have been a temptation on the part of some to participate in cultic worship, with either their Jewish or Gentile contemporaries. Christianity, after all, was still in its infancy.

It is against this background that the emphasis of Hebrews on priesthood and cult begins to make sense. Aware of the difficulties described above, Hebrews reminds its readers that they have a high priest, a temple cult, and a sacrificial offering, but this offering, cult, and priest are not on earth. Their high priest is Jesus Christ who passed into the heavenly sanctuary at the moment of his death, and their sacrificial offering is the death of this priest who atoned for sins, once and for all. Thus there is no further need for a cultic priesthood or a temple where sacrifices are offered daily.

The high priestly theology of Hebrews is rooted in the cross of Jesus Christ. Although the author speaks of priests, sanctuaries, and cultic offerings, his eyes are fixed on the cross of Jesus. In the cross, he sees the altar of sacrifice and the way into the heavenly sanctuary. On the cross, he sees a great high priest according to the order of Melchizedck. One might say, that the paradox of Hebrews is that it is simultaneously the most secular and cultic writing of the New Testament. It is the most cultic because of its extended discussion about priesthood and sacrifice. It is the most secular because this discussion centers on the death of one whom the world executed as a criminal. In other words, the cultic theology of Hebrews is a profound meditation on the meaning of Christ's shameful death on the cross.

Those who preach from Hebrews need to bring these paradoxes to their congregations in order to remind them of the profound mystery of their faith. Like the author of Hebrews, preachers must reflect on the most secular of all events, the condemnation and death of one whom the world judged to be a criminal.

Paul in Ordinary Time

Year C

During the course of Year C the Lectionary draws from the following Pauline letters: 1 Corinthians, Galatians, Colossians, Philemon, 1 and 2 Timothy, and 2 Thessalonians. The Lectionary also makes use of Hebrews, which will be considered in this chapter because of its importance and the traditional understanding of Hebrews as Pauline in the Church of the East.

Year C makes use of six Pauline letters that do not appear in the other cycles: Galatians, Colossians, Philemon, 1 and 2 Timothy, and 2 Thessalonians. Of these letters, Galatians is the most powerful and dramatic and provides preachers with another opportunity to discuss Paul's teaching on justification by faith. Philemon is the briefest of Paul's letters, but it raises an important issue: the manner in which Christ alters the relationship of believers to each other. Scholars generally classify Colossians, 1 and 2 Timothy, and 2 Thessalonians as deutero-Pauline because they suspect that others wrote them in Paul's name. Even if these letters are deutero-Pauline, each contains important teaching on Christ and the moral life. During Year C, therefore, preachers have an opportunity to preach from a variety of Pauline writings.

1 Corinthians

Year C begins with seven readings from 1 Corinthians. Since 1 Corinthians occurs eight times in Year A and five in Year B, the Sunday Lectionary draws upon this letter twenty times in its three-year cycle. 1 Corinthians also occurs at the beginning of each liturgical cycle. This position and its frequent use indicate its importance for preaching.

The literary context. During Year A, the Lectionary drew from chapters 1–4, Paul's discussion about factions and divisions within the Corinthian church. During Year B, the readings came from chapters 6–10, in which Paul dealt with questions concerning immorality, marriage, and participation in cultic banquets at which the food had been sacrificed to idols. In Year C, the Lectionary focuses on chapter 12, which deals with the gifts of the Spirit, and chapter 15, which presents Paul's teaching on the resurrection of the dead. While each chapter may appear to be a self-contained unit, both belong to the same literary context in which Paul discusses problems and questions raised by the Corinthian church.

Chapter 12 is part of Paul's answer to a letter which the Corinthians had sent him, as is evident from the opening verse, "Now in regard to spiritual gifts, . . ." (12:1). A similar and even more explicit formula occurs in 7:1, "Now in regard to the matters *about which you wrote.*" Having employed this explicit formula in 7:1, Paul uses an abbreviated formula in 12:1 to indicate that this material is also his answer to a letter from the Corinthians.

In that letter the Corinthians had raised a number of questions about marriage and sexual abstinence (chapter 7), as well as the advisability of sharing in cultic banquets (chapters 8–10). In addition to these issues, their letter raised questions about the gifts of the Spirit. For example, what is the more desirable gift? Speaking in tongues or prophesying?

The issue was important because the Corinthian community was generously endowed with the gifts of the Spirit (see 1:4-7). However, the Corinthians were still immature in their faith and did not understand that the gifts of the Spirit are for building up the Church and not for personal edification. Consequently, some prized their gifts, especially the gift of tongues, as more important than other gifts such as prophecy.

Afraid that this might lead to division and strife, in chapters 12–14 Paul explains the origin, purpose, and relative importance of various spiritual gifts. Their origin is the Spirit; their purpose is to edify the Church; and their importance is determined in light of the contribution each makes to building up the Church. In chapter 12, therefore, Paul addresses the issue of unity and diversity. There are many gifts but all come from the same Spirit. There is one body, but it has many members, all with their own gifts.

On first reading Paul's praise of love in chapter 13 appears unrelated to what precedes and follows. In fact, it is an integral part of Paul's rhetorical strategy which is to show the Corinthians that even though there are different spiritual gifts, everyone can pursue love which is the most important and lasting gift. Love is the more excellent way.

Having explained the surpassing importance of love, Paul returns to his discussion of spiritual gifts in chapter 14. In this chapter, which does not occur in the Sunday Lectionary, he discusses the relationship between the gift of tongues and the gift of prophecy. He argues that the gift of prophecy is more important than the gift of tongues because those who prophesy interpret what is said by those who speak in tongues. Thus, Paul valued those gifts as most beneficial that build up and edify the Christian community. Spiritual gifts that do not build up or edify the community are less important, no matter how impressive their outward manifestation. In working through this section, preachers should make a concerted effort to show how the gifts of the Spirit are related to the common good of the community.

Chapter 15 is Paul's most detailed discussion of the resurrection of the dead. The occasion for this chapter is the claim, on the part of some, that there is no resurrection of the dead (see 15:12). In the first half of the chapter, Paul reminds the Corinthians of the gospel he preached to them, a gospel in which Christ's resurrection plays a central role (15:1-11). Then, on the basis of Christ's resurrection, he argues for the general resurrection of the dead (15:12-34). In the final portion of the chapter, he discusses the nature of the resurrection body (15:35-58).

Paul's discussion about the resurrection may seem strange to believers who take this teaching for granted. The resurrection of the dead, however, was not immediately obvious to Paul's Corinthian converts, many of whom viewed their new faith as another form of philosophy or wisdom. This is why some understood the resurrection in purely spiritual terms and mistakenly thought they had already been raised up in Christ. Accordingly, it was necessary for Paul to provide them with further teaching about the resurrection to show that Christ's resurrection was not an isolated event. Rather, it was the beginning of the general resurrection of the dead, for, what happened to Christ will happen to all who believe in him.

Strategy: The Text in Its Context

The Same Spirit
Second Sunday: 1 Cor 12:4-11

This text is the beginning of Paul's discussion about the gifts of the Spirit, which will continue throughout chapters 12–14. He begins with a general discussion about the gifts of the Spirit to show that the same Spirit produces the different spiritual gifts that the Corinthians enjoy. This will allow him to argue in next week's reading (12:12-30) that the diverse gifts of the Spirit are meant for the common good of the body, which is the Church.

While segments of the contemporary Church have experienced a charismatic renewal, the experience of the Spirit was central to the life of the whole Church for Paul. Thus, the entire Church, not a portion of it, was charismatic. It was this experience of the Spirit more than anything else that convinced believers that Christ was risen and alive. Thus, even though Paul's Gentile converts had not seen the Risen Lord, they experienced his Spirit, the Spirit of the living God.

The Corinthians prized the more dramatic aspects of the Spirit such as the gift of tongues, an inarticulate and frenzied speech which they viewed as participation in the language of angels. Paul acknowledged the gift and even claimed it for himself (see 14:18), but he knew that there were less dramatic gifts that were more important because they were more effective in building up the Church. In addition to the gift of tongues, he lists wisdom, knowledge, faith, healing, mighty deeds, prophecy, the discernment of spirits, and the interpretation of tongues.

The emphatic manner in which Paul identifies the same Spirit as the origin of these many gifts (see the beginning and the end of this reading) suggests that the Corinthians, whose faith was still immature, may have thought that a variety of spirits produced these many gifts. For Paul this could not be. Just as there is only one God who is the Father of all, and one Lord who is Jesus the Christ, so there is only one Spirit, the Spirit of the Risen Lord and the living God. From this one Spirit comes a variety of gifts essential to the life of the Church.

Although it is easy for contemporary believers to confess that there is only one Spirit, many no longer experience this Spirit, and few think of themselves as possessing the gifts of the Spirit, except in some formal way. For Paul, however, the experience of the Spirit was vital to the Church. Without the Spirit, there are no gifts, and without the gifts of the Spirit the Church cannot function as the body of Christ.

This reading challenges preachers to rethink the role of the Spirit and its gifts for contemporary Christianity. Those who preach from it might begin by analyzing the congregation. What are the manifestations of the Spirit in the congregation? If the answer is not immediately obvious, this may indicate that the congregation needs to rekindle the gifts of the Spirit for the common good of the Church.

One Body, Many Members
Third Sunday: 1 Cor 12:12-30

Having shown the Corinthians that their many gifts come from the same Spirit (12:4-11), Paul employs the metaphor of the body to explain how these diverse gifts function within the Church. This metaphor would have been familiar to Paul's contemporaries since Greek and Roman philosophers employed it to explain the role of citizens in civil society. Paul, however, goes a step further and develops this metaphor in relationship to Christ. He shows that in addition to being a body with parts that function differently for the good of the whole, the Corinthians are one body in Christ because each one was baptized into one Spirit. Thus the Corinthians should think of the body which they form as the body of Christ since each of them has been baptized into it.

Preachers should not overlook the role that the Spirit plays in this reading since references to the Spirit clearly relate it to last week's text. Thus, Paul affirms that it was in one Spirit that the Corinthians were baptized into one body, and they all drink of the one Spirit, a reference to the Eucharist. The many gifts of the Spirit, then, are intended for the Church which is like a body, the body of Christ.

The reading begins by explaining the metaphor that Paul will develop: although a body has many parts, these parts form one body (vv. 12-13). Next he illustrates the metaphor with a number of practical examples to show that even though some parts may seem more important than others, the body needs all of its parts to function properly (vv. 14-26). Finally, Paul applies the text to the situation of the Corinthians who have not understood that their many spiritual gifts are intended for the good of the whole body (vv. 27-31). In this application he notes that they are a body in Christ, and each one is a part of that body. In light of what Paul has just said, it should be obvious to them that their diverse gifts are meant for the whole Church.

Paul concludes with a list of ministries within the Church, beginning with the most important: apostles, prophets, teachers, mighty deeds or miracle workers, healers, administrators, and those who speak in tongues. The ministry of those who speak in tongues occurs at the end of the list since, as Paul will argue in chapter 14, this ministry does not build up the Church unless there is a prophet to interpret what is said.

Diversity is a perennial challenge for the Church. On the one hand, there is a subtle temptation to extol one's gifts to the detriment of others. On the other, there is a temptation to mute the diversity of the Church for the sake of uniformity. For Paul, however, unity and diversity are inseparable since the unity of the Church derives from the same Spirit who dispenses a variety of gifts. A Church without diversity would be like a body without parts; it would not be the body of Christ. Likewise, a diverse Church without a source of unity would be a body without a common purpose, a body that could not function. The perennial challenge of the Church is to maintain the unity of the Spirit without extinguishing the diversity that has its origin in the *same* Spirit.

A More Excellent Way
Fourth Sunday: 1 Cor 12:31–13:13

Having explained that the same Spirit is the source of all spiritual gifts and that these gifts are destined for the good of the body which is the Church, Paul encourages the Corinthians to strive for the greater spiritual gifts. Aware that his immature community is attracted to more spectacular gifts such as speaking in tongues, he encourages the Corinthians to adopt a more excellent way that is accessible to all, the way of love.

On first reading, it may appear that this passage is unrelated to what Paul has said and will say in chapter 14. A closer examination, however, reveals that this text plays a crucial role in Paul's discussion about the gifts of the Spirit.

12:1-31	Many gifts from the same Spirit *build up* the one body which is *the Church.*
12:31–13:13	Love is the more excellent way which surpasses all of these gifts.
14:1-40	Prophecy is more beneficial than tongues because it *builds up the Church.*

The primary role of 12:31–13:13 is to show that without love the gifts of the Spirit will not function as they ought within the community of the Church; for while spiritual gifts such as tongues build up the individual in the eyes of others, without love they do not build up the body of Christ which is the Church.

In the first part of this passage (vv. 1-3), Paul lists several of the gifts that he discussed in chapter 12: tongues, prophecy, knowledge, and faith. In every instance he affirms that without love these gifts are of no avail. Having argued that love is indispensable, he employs a number of positive and negative statements to explain what he means by love (vv. 4-6). Finally, he compares love with the gifts of prophecy, tongues, and knowledge and concludes that whereas these gifts will fail, love will endure (vv. 8-13).

Having explained the surpassing importance of love, in chapter 14 Paul argues that the gift of prophecy will be more beneficial to the Corinthians than the gift of tongues since prophetic instruction builds up the community whereas the inarticulate speech of those who speak in tongues does not. Thus the chapter begins, "Pursue love, but strive eagerly for the spiritual gifts, above all that you may prophesy" (14:1).

Those who choose to preach from this passage may find the task more difficult than they anticipate because the text is so familiar and is often isolated from its context. The wider context of chapters 12–14, however, shows that Paul's purpose is to build up the body, which is the Church.

Because this wider context deals with building up the Church, Paul's discussion about love has an ecclesial dimension. The love he extols builds up the body of Christ. Without such love, the community cannot exist, no matter how many gifts it possesses. This love is patterned after the self-sacrificing love of Christ who gave himself for the Church and finds its fullest expression within an ecclesial context. For this reason, those who preach from this text should strive to relate Paul's teaching on love to the daily life of the Church.

The Gospel Paul Preaches
Fifth Sunday: 1 Cor 15:1-11

For the next four weeks, the Lectionary's readings will come from 1 Corinthians 15. The extensive use of this chapter, which the Lectionary also draws upon in Year A for the Feast of Christ the King, is extraordinary. Only Romans 8 occurs as frequently. It is imperative, therefore, that preachers be thoroughly familiar with the structure and argument of this chapter.

The occasion of the chapter is a problem within the Corinthian community. Some members of the Corinthian church were saying that there is no resurrection of the dead (15:12; see 2 Tim 2:16-18 for a similar problem). Having experienced the power of the Spirit in their lives, some mistakenly thought that they already enjoyed the fullness of salvation. Thus, they viewed themselves as raised up in Christ. There would be no bodily resurrection, a notion which many of the Corinthians confused with resuscitation, and so found repulsive. To their way of thinking, it was the person's spirit that was important. If the spirit is raised up by the power of God's Spirit, then a person is saved.

In chapter 15 Paul finds it necessary to remind the Corinthians of the central message of the gospel he preaches: Christ has been raised from the dead. He does this in three steps. First, he reminds the Corinthians of the gospel he preached to them (vv. 1-11). Second, on the basis of this he argues that there will be a resurrection of the dead (vv. 12-34). Third, he explains what he means by the resurrection body and describes how the dead will be raised (vv. 35-58).

The reading for this week provides the foundation for the argument that Paul will make in the rest of chapter 15: there will be a general resurrection of the dead. To make that argument Paul must show the Corinthians that there is an intimate connection between the resurrection of Christ and the general resurrection of all believers, an event that will occur at Christ's parousia. In effect, Paul argues that Christ's resurrection was the beginning of the general resurrection of the dead. Consequently, if there is no resurrection of the dead, then not even Christ has been raised from the dead. The reading for this week can be structured as follows.

15:1-2   Introduction.
15:3-5   The essential content of the gospel.
15:6-10   Witnesses to the Risen Lord.
15:11   The common witness to the resurrection.

In the introductory verses (vv. 1-2) Paul reminds the Corinthians of the gospel which effects salvation, provided that they firmly hold to the original message he preached. In vv. 3-5, Paul provides a summary of that gospel. He himself received this summary of the gospel and faithfully preached it to the Corinthians.

• Christ died for sins in accordance with the Scriptures.
• Christ was buried.

- Christ was raised on the third day in accordance with the Scriptures.
- He then appeared to Kephas and the Twelve.

The gospel Paul handed on to the Corinthians is the good news of Christ's saving death and resurrection which happened in accordance with God's will, effected the forgiveness of sins, and is attested to by Kephas (Peter) and the other members of the Twelve.

Having reminded them of this gospel, in vv. 6-10 Paul provides an extensive list of witnesses to whom the Risen Christ appeared in addition to Peter and the Twelve: a group of five hundred, James, then all of the apostles (Paul uses the term in a broad sense that goes beyond the Twelve). Finally, Paul includes himself. The Risen Lord appeared to him (see Acts 9; Gal 1:15-16), even though he had persecuted the Church. Thus, there is an extensive list of witnesses to whom the Risen Lord appeared.

Paul concludes by emphasizing that all of the apostles preach the same gospel (v. 11). The resurrection of Christ is not peculiar to his gospel. It is the preaching of the entire Church that cannot be compromised without destroying the gospel the Church preaches.

This text offers preachers an opportunity to remind their congregations of what is at the heart of the gospel the Church proclaims: the saving death and resurrection of Christ which has been faithfully handed on from one believing generation to the next. If believers focused upon this saving message and its implications, perhaps there would be fewer divisions within the Church. For, while believers need not always agree with each other on matters of policy, they must agree with each other about the gospel they have received and proclaim.

Christ Has Been Raised
Sixth Sunday: 1 Cor 15:12, 16-20

This reading is Paul's response to those who say that there is no resurrection of the dead. To appreciate his argument preachers should read the whole of vv. 12-34 since the Lectionary only provides part of Paul's argument.

Paul's line of reasoning can be summarized as follows. In vv. 13-19 he draws out the logical consequences of the premise that there is no resurrection of the dead. If there is no resurrection of the dead, then not even Christ has been raised from the dead. If Christ has not been raised, their faith is empty. If Christ has not been raised, the apostles are false witnesses since they testify that he has been raised. And, if the dead have not been raised, the Corinthians are still in their sins. They are the most pitiable of people.

Having drawn out the absurd consequences that flow from the Corinthian position that there is no resurrection of the dead, in vv. 20-28, Paul then goes on to spell out the consequences of his gospel that Christ has indeed been raised from the dead. Namely, Christ is the first fruits of those who will be raised from the dead: what happened to him will happen to all believers. Since death entered the world through a human being, Adam, the resurrection of the dead comes through a human being, Christ, the new Adam. Everything, however, occurs in an orderly fashion. First, Christ is raised, then at his parousia the dead will be raised with him. Christ will then hand over everything to God the Father. Death will be defeated, all things will be subjected to God, and God will be all in all.

In vv. 29-34 Paul concludes with some practical arguments. Referring to a practice in the Corinthian community of baptizing people on behalf of the dead, he asks why they do this if there is no resurrection of the dead. Finally, pointing to himself and other preachers, he asks why they sacrifice themselves if there is no resurrection of the dead. They would do better to eat, drink, and be merry if there is no resurrection of the dead.

The Corinthian position, that there is no resurrection of the dead, may seem strange to contemporary believers who regularly proclaim their faith in the resurrection of Christ and the bodily resurrection of the dead. On the pastoral level, however, a similar problem arises whenever contemporary believers live as though there will be no resurrection of the dead. For example, when contemporary believers view this life as the fullness of life, they deny the resurrection of the dead on a practical level. This text challenges preachers to draw out the practical implications of faith in Christ's resurrection. Those who believe that he has been raised, also believe that they will be raised from the dead. Consequently, they no longer live for this life only.

The Image of Christ
Seventh Sunday: 1 Cor 15:45-49

This brief reading, heard apart from its context, will make little sense to most congregations unless preachers provide some background. The background begins with questions that Paul himself poses, "But someone may say, 'How are the dead raised? With what kind of body will they come back?'" These questions suggest that part of the problem at Corinth was a misunderstanding of the resurrection body. Whereas Paul viewed resurrection as transformation, many of the Corinthians understood the resurrection of the dead as bodily resuscitation: a return to one's former state of life.

Paul did not view the resurrection of the dead in this way. Thus in the second part of chapter 15, he turns his attention to the nature of the resurrection body and explains how the dead will be raised. To make sense of the text preachers must familiarize themselves with Paul's line of argument in 15:35-58.

Paul begins with an example from nature (vv. 36-41). There is a difference between what one sows and what one reaps. There is also a difference between various kinds of flesh (human beings, animals, birds, fish). Finally, there are even differences among the heavenly bodies such as the moon and the stars. Each has its own brightness.

Having established that there are such differences in nature, in vv. 42-44 Paul applies the comparison to the question of the resurrection body. Just as there are differences in nature, so there is a difference between the earthly body and the resurrection body. The first is corruptible, dishonorable, and weak, but it will be raised up and transformed into a body that is incorruptible, honorable, and powerful. Sown in death as a natural body, it will be raised as a spiritual body.

It is at this point that the reading for this week, a comparison between Adam and Christ, makes its appearance (vv. 45-

49). Adam was the first man, the one into whom God breathed a life-giving spirit. Thus he became the ancestor of all human beings. However, just as Adam was formed from the earth, so were his descendants. The body each possesses is an earthly body in the image of Adam.

In contrast to Adam, Christ is the heavenly man who has been raised from the dead. He is the new Adam whose body was changed and transformed by the power of the resurrection. Just as we now bear the image of the earthly one (Adam), so we will bear the image of the heavenly one (Christ), when our bodies are raised and transformed after the pattern of Christ's resurrected body at the general resurrection of the dead.

This is a challenging reading to preach, but it can be very rewarding. For, while contemporary believers dutifully profess their faith in the resurrection of the dead, most are puzzled, as were the Corinthians. What does it mean to say that we will be raised on the last day? Paul's answer is "transformation." The earthly body will be changed and transformed after the pattern of the risen Lord. The body will not be left behind, but neither will it be exactly the same. It will be changed and transformed in a way we cannot imagine but which we anticipate whenever we profess our faith in the Risen Christ.

God's Final Victory
Eighth Sunday: 1 Cor 15:54-58

This reading is the climax of Paul's argument on behalf of the resurrection of the dead. Having reminded the Corinthians of the gospel he preached among them (vv. 1-11), and having explained that there will be a resurrection of the dead (vv. 12-34) and what he means by a resurrection body (vv. 35-49), Paul describes what will happen at the resurrection of the dead. The scenario he envisions includes the parousia since that is when the general resurrection of the dead will occur in conjunction with Christ's return. Some believers will still be alive when Christ returns, but they will be immediately changed, for the earthly body will be transformed into a heavenly or resurrection body. As for the dead, they will be raised incorruptible. When the bodies of the living and the dead have been transformed, then death will be swallowed up in victory, for neither the living nor the dead will be under the power of death.

This text, much of which will be familiar to those who have heard Handel's *Messiah*, proclaims God's final victory through Jesus Christ. Because it does, it provides preachers with an opportunity to give their congregations a glimpse of what lies ahead: God's final victory over death. In effect, the text proclaims that there will be a final triumph of God in which Christ will play the decisive role. Faith in, and hope for, this final victory puts everything in perspective. It reminds believers that God will be victorious over the powers of sin and death, and God will be all in all.

Strategy: Theological Themes

These readings from 1 Corinthians center on two themes: (1) the Church as a Spirit-endowed community, (2) the resurrection of the dead. Consequently, even if preachers do not preach from these Pauline texts every week, they can and should develop these themes.

The Church as a Spirit-endowed Community

Whereas contemporary Christians often look askance at charismatic manifestations, Paul assumed that his communities would experience the gifts of God's Spirit in a lively way. In 1 Thess 5:19, for example, he warns, "Do not quench the Spirit," and in Gal 3:1-6, he points to the presence of the Spirit as an indication that the Galatians have been justified.

The Corinthian community was abundantly endowed with spiritual gifts so that Paul could write, ". . . you are not lacking in any spiritual gift as you wait for the revelation of our Lord Jesus Christ" (1 Cor 1:7). In the case of the Corinthians, however, there was need for balance and maturity. Having been endowed with so many spiritual gifts, some mistakenly thought they already enjoyed the fullness of salvation and were tempted to view certain gifts as more prestigious than others. Thus, it was necessary for Paul to place the gifts of the Spirit in perspective and remind the Corinthians that their gifts were for the benefit of the whole community, and that love was the more excellent way.

The problems occasioned by the gifts of the Spirit at Corinth are not the problems of most congregations today. In many instances, the problem is that the Spirit has been extinguished. 1 Corinthians provides preachers with an opportunity to speak of the Spirit once more and rekindle that powerful flame.

The Resurrection of the Dead

Some teachings are so central to Christianity that they are taken for granted. Paul's teaching on the resurrection of the dead is among these. Week after week, the congregation proclaims, "Christ has died, Christ is risen, Christ will come again." Every Sunday it professes its faith in the resurrection of the dead. Unfortunately, the practical life of believers does not always correspond to the faith they profess. Because they live in a secular society, it is easy for believers to view the comfortable life as the fullness of life.

Paul would have none of this. Although he proclaimed the victory of Christ's death and resurrection, he knew that the final triumph of God had not yet occurred. This victory will only come at the parousia, when the dead will be raised incorruptible and God will be all in all.

1 Corinthians provides preachers with an opportunity to develop the theme of the general resurrection of the dead. In doing so, the focus should be upon God's final victory in Christ. Something has already happened in Christ, for believers do enjoy the gift of the Spirit within the community of the Church. But the final victory lies ahead, and it will not occur until the power of death has been defeated at the general resurrection of the dead. When that happens, believers will share in Christ's resurrection, and God will be all in all.

Galatians

The Lectionary draws upon Galatians for six weeks during Year C, but none of its selections is very long. Nevertheless, they are significant passages from five of the letter's six chapters and, when read in context, these afford preachers an opportunity to say something about the entire letter.

This letter has played an important role in the history of the Church because of its teaching on justification by faith. Augustine, Chrysostom, Aquinas, Luther, and Calvin wrote important commentaries on this letter, in part, because of its teaching on justification. What Paul says about justification in Galatians, however, is difficult to grasp since he was not presenting a dispassionate account of his teaching but responding to opponents who questioned his apostleship and mission among the Gentiles. Consequently, the letter is sharp and polemical in tone as Paul defends "the truth of the gospel" (2:5, 14). To understand the argument of Galatians and appreciate how the Lectionary readings function, it is necessary to say something about the letter's background and structure.

Strategy: Understanding the Context

The historical context. Galatians is Paul's response to a crisis. Having established a number of communities in Galatia (a Roman province in what is modern-day Turkey), he moved on. Shortly after his departure, Jewish Christian missionaries came to the churches Paul had established and taught the Galatians that if they wished to be numbered among Abraham's descendants and share in the benefits of Israel's Messiah they must have themselves circumcised and do the works of the Mosaic Law, especially its dietary prescriptions and Sabbath observance.

In contrast to these missionaries, Paul did not require the Galatians to be circumcised or adopt a Jewish way of life. His conversion experience taught him that God had done something new in Christ which the Mosaic Law could not accomplish: it effected life-giving righteousness through the death and resurrection of Christ. Thus Paul writes, "for if justification comes through the law, then Christ died for nothing" (2:21). And again, "For if a law had been given that could bring life, then righteousness would in reality come from the law" (3:21). From Paul's perspective, the Gentile Galatians, who were expe-

riencing the gift of God's Spirit (3:1-6), were already Abraham's
descendants because they belonged to his singular descendant,
the Christ (3:29).

Nothing less than the truth of the gospel was at stake in the
crisis at Galatia (2:5, 14); namely, God does not justify a person
on the basis of doing the works of the Law but on the basis of
trusting faith in what he has accomplished through the death
and resurrection of his Son. Consequently, Paul argued that it is
not necessary for Gentiles to adopt a Jewish way of life. They
are already Abraham's descendants in Christ because they belong to Abraham's singular descendant, the Christ. What the
Gentiles must do is persevere in their trusting faith and live according to the urging of God's Spirit.

Galatians, then, is a letter in which Paul argues that it is not
necessary to do something above and beyond what God has
done. God has accomplished the work of salvation, and the
proper response of the justified is trusting faith in Christ.

For contemporary readers, it may seem strange and un-
seemly that there were such disputes between Paul and other
Christian missionaries about the significance of what God had
done in Christ. It is important to remember, however, that Galatians stands at an early stage of doctrinal development when believers were still trying to grasp the full meaning of Christ's
saving death and resurrection. Those who objected to Paul's
preaching were sincere believers, but they did not understand
the full meaning of what God had done in Christ. In contrast to
them, Paul realized that God had effected something in Christ
which the Mosaic Law could not: life-giving righteousness. It
was in light of the controversy at Galatia that Paul formulated,
perhaps for the first time, his teaching on justification by faith
apart from the Law.

The literary context. Apart from its introduction (1:1-10) and
conclusion (6:11-18), Galatians consists of three parts: an autobiographical statement in which Paul defends the circumcision-
free gospel he preaches among the Gentiles (1:11–2:21); a
personal and exegetical defense of "the truth of the gospel"
(3:1–5:12); and an exhortation to live by the Spirit (5:13–6:10).

In his introductory remarks (1:1-10), Paul already signals what he will argue in the rest of the letter: (1) his apostleship did not come from human beings but through Jesus Christ and God the Father; (2) Christ freely gave himself to free us from "the present evil age"; and those who are disturbing the Galatians are perverting the gospel.

Having put the Galatians on notice in this introductory statement, Paul employs an extended autobiographical statement to show that the gospel he preaches is not of human origin but was revealed to him when God called him to be an apostle to the Gentiles (1:11–2:21). Accordingly, Paul recounts his former life as a persecutor of the Church, his call or conversion experience, his first visit to Jerusalem, the time he spent in Syria and Cilicia, his second visit to Jerusalem, and the controversy at Antioch. He employs this autobiographical material to show the Galatians that (1) his circumcision-free gospel is rooted in the call that made him an apostle to the Gentiles, (2) the church at Jerusalem acknowledged the divine origin of his ministry among the Gentiles, and (3) he defended "the truth of the gospel" at Antioch whereas Peter, Barnabas, and other Jewish Christian believers compromised it. This part of the letter concludes with a careful statement of what Paul means by "the truth of the gospel"; namely, a person is justified by faith apart from doing the works of the Law (see 2:15-21).

The second part of Galatians (3:1–5:12) presents an extended defense of "truth of the gospel." Paul's argument depends, in great measure, on his reading of scripture in light of what God has done in Christ. His major points can be summarized as follows:

- Since the Galatians already experience the gift of God's Spirit, there is no need for them to be circumcised and adopt a Jewish way of life. They are in the correct relationship to God, for they have been justified through the gift of God's Spirit.
- Since the Galatians have been baptized into Christ who is Abraham's singular descendant, they are Abraham's children in Christ. There is no need for them to have themselves circumcised.

- The Law had a limited role in God's plan of salvation. It served as Israel's "disciplinarian" during the period of Israel's legal minority. Now that Christ has come, the Law's role in salvation history has ended.
- If the Galatians adopt a Jewish way of life, they will return to the stage of legal minority and slavery rather than inherit the promise given to Abraham's descendants.
- The Galatians belong to the line of descent that issues from the free woman Sarah and her son Isaac. In contrast to them, those who are urging the Galatians to be circumcised belong to the line of descent that issues from the slave woman Hagar and her son Ishmael.
- If the Galatians have themselves circumcised and adopt a Jewish way of life, Christ will be of no benefit to them. They will have nullified God's grace.

Having made his argument for "the truth of the gospel," Paul, in the final part of the letter (5:13–6:10), exhorts the Galatians to live according to the urging of the Spirit. For many readers, this part of the letter may seem anti-climatic and even contradictory. This moral exhortation, however, is central to Paul's argument; for, having told the Galatians that they are no longer under the law, it might appear that there is no room for the moral life in Paul's law-free gospel. Nothing could be further from the truth. Although the Galatians are no longer under the law, they fulfill it through the love commandment. Empowered by the Spirit, they fulfill what the Law requires by serving each other in love, the sacrificial love that Christ manifested on the cross.

The letter concludes with a summary of Paul's argument (6:11-18). Because of what God has effected in Christ, neither circumcision nor uncircumcision matters. What matters is being a new creation in Christ. Those who belong to this new creation are "the Israel of God" (6:16).

Apostleship from God and Christ
Ninth Sunday: Gal 1:1-2, 6-10

These verses are the beginning of Paul's letter to the Galatians. They consist of a greeting (vv. 1-5) and a statement of astonishment (vv. 6-10). The Lectionary does not produce the whole of Paul's greeting, omitting vv. 4-5, in which he makes an important statement about Jesus Christ "who gave himself for our sins that he might rescue us from the present evil age." Nonetheless, few readers will miss Paul's point. He did not receive his apostleship from, or through, human beings but through Jesus Christ and God who raised him from the dead. Paul, of course, is referring to his call and conversion, the focus of next week's reading.

When compared to the greetings of Paul's other letters, the greeting of Galatians is remarkable for its length and the adamant manner in which Paul insists on the divine origin of his apostleship. He puts the Galatians on notice that his apostleship originated in Christ and God. He was not ordained or commissioned by others to fulfill the ministry he carried out among them. In next week's reading Paul will say something similar about the gospel that he preaches among the Gentiles, thereby establishing the divine origin of his gospel as well as of his apostolic office (see 1:11).

After this greeting, Paul expresses his amazement that the Galatians are so quickly forsaking the gospel he preached to them. This statement must have taken the Galatians by surprise since, at this point, Paul's letters normally include a thanksgiving prayer in which he prays for the recipients of the letter and thanks God for the blessings bestowed upon them. The absence of such a prayer and the unexpected presence of this statement of astonishment indicate that something is wrong.

The problem is that other preachers have come to Galatia and disturbed Paul's converts by proclaiming a message that he identifies as a perversion of the gospel because it would require the Galatians to become circumcised and do the works of the Mosaic Law, in addition to believing in what God has done in Christ. In effect, the agitators were calling into question the sufficiency of the Christ event. Nothing less than the truth of the gospel was at stake.

This text is a marvelous example of Paul's passion for the truth of the gospel that can be summarized as follows: "A person is not justified by works of the law but through faith in Jesus

Christ" (2:16). Because Paul's apostleship has its origin in Christ and God, the Galatians can rely on the gospel he preached to them. To be sure, the gospel can be proclaimed by other apostles, but it must never be compromised. It may be expressed in different terms, but anything that questions the sufficiency of what God has done in Christ is a perversion of the gospel.

While congregations will sense the emotion and urgency expressed in this text, most will not understand why Paul writes as he does. Therefore, preachers must say something about the problem he faced at Galatia. This background need not be technical or extensive, but it should explain the crisis Paul faced (some were questioning the gospel he preached), his response (faith in Christ is the foundation of the gospel), and what was at stake (the truth of the gospel). Such a homily will summarize the central message of Galatians and prepare the congregation for the readings that follow.

Gospel and Call
Tenth Sunday: 1:11-19

Last week's reading focused on the divine origin of Paul's apostleship and the danger presented by preachers who, in Paul's view, were perverting the gospel he had preached to the Galatians. In this week's reading, the focus turns to Paul's gospel. Just as he did not receive his apostleship from or through human beings (1:1), so he did not receive, nor was he taught, the gospel he preaches among the Gentiles. Rather, "it came through a revelation of Jesus Christ" (1:12).

This revelation of Jesus Christ refers to Paul's call or conversion, which Luke describes three times in the Acts of the Apostles (chapters 9, 22, 26). Paul's own account of his call does not contain the narrative detail of Acts, but he and Luke agree on the central point. Although Paul was once zealous for the Law and persecuted the Church, he was called to preach the gospel he once persecuted to the Gentiles. The reading has several parts: the origin of Paul's gospel; an account of his former way of life; his call to be the Apostle to the Gentiles; Paul's first visit to Jerusalem three years after his call.

Paul's insistence that his gospel came from a revelation of Jesus Christ, like his affirmation that his apostleship is of divine origin, is essential to the argument he makes to the Galatians. For, if human beings had appointed him to preach the gospel and taught him what to say, then the agitators could say to the Galatians, "When Paul preached the gospel without requiring you to be circumcised, he went beyond what he was taught and appointed to do." But, if Paul's gospel and apostleship originated in God and Christ, then the circumcision-free gospel he preaches among the Gentiles is of divine origin.

To establish the divine origin of his gospel, Paul recounts his former way of life and the call that made him the Apostle to the Gentiles. As regards his past, he insists on his zealousness for the Law that led him to persecute Christians for doing what he himself now does: preaching the gospel to Gentiles without requiring them to adopt a Jewish way of life as prescribed in the Mosaic Law. By recalling his former zealousness for the law, Paul does more than affirm his Jewish ancestry. He implies that something must have occurred to account for his present behavior.

The dramatic event to which Paul alludes is his call or conversion. Employing language reminiscent of the call of Jeremiah (Jer 1:4-10) and of the Servant in Isaiah (Isa 49:1-6), Paul describes his conversion in terms of a prophetic call. Before he was born, God graciously called him to preach to the Gentiles by revealing his Son to him.

The essence of God's revelation to Paul was that the crucified Jesus was the Son of God. Previous to his call/conversion the very concept of a crucified Messiah was a contradiction in terms to Paul; for, Deut 21:23 (quoted in Gal 3:13) identifies those who hang on a tree (those who are crucified) as being under God's curse. Paul's pre-conversion evaluation of Jesus, then, can be put summarized in a syllogism. The Law identifies those who hang on a tree as under God's curse (see Deut 21:23). Jesus hung on a tree, for he was crucified. *Therefore*, Jesus was under God's curse!

What happened on the road to Damascus not only contradicted what Paul thought of Jesus, it put into question his understanding of the Law. In effect, Paul had misunderstood the Law when he persecuted the followers of the crucified Messiah. He now realized that God had called him to preach Christ among the Gentiles without requiring them to be circumcised. The meaning of this revelation was clear, and there was no need for him to go to Jerusalem for an interpretation or clarification. He knew and understood what the revelation meant. Therefore, he went to Arabia to preach the gospel to the Gentiles, and then returned to Damascus.

Three years later, Paul went to Jerusalem to confer with Kephas (Peter). The meeting was brief and lasted only fifteen days. He did not see the other apostles. In effect, Paul is suggesting that the Jerusalem church did not commission him or teach him the gospel. He had already been preaching the circumcision-free gospel among Gentiles in Arabia for three years. Accordingly, Paul's apostleship and gospel have their origin in God, and the Galatians should trust him rather than the agitators.

Paul remains a mystery to most believers, especially Catholics. He seems arrogant, self-assured, and judgmental. This text provides an opportunity to dispel this view of Paul because it shows that his self-assurance is rooted in a divine call which made him the Apostle to the Gentiles. He is not simply another evangelist; he is Christ's Apostle, the one whom God has chosen to bring the circumcision-free gospel to the Gentiles. It was Paul who most clearly understood the implications of the Christ event and made it possible for Gentiles to share in the benefits of Israel's Messiah. This is why the Church reads his letters as inspired Scripture and why we must wrestle with his thought rather than simply dismiss it.

Justified by Faith
Eleventh Sunday: Gal 2:16, 19-21

With this passage, we arrive at Paul's most explicit statement of justification by faith. If preachers intend to say anything at all about Galatians, they should focus on this text.

Having recounted how he received his gospel when God revealed his Son to him (1:13-24), Paul narrates two more episodes from his past to persuade the Galatians of the truth of the gospel he preached to them. Since neither episode occurs in the Lectionary readings, it is important for preachers to be familiar with them.

The first is Paul's second visit to Jerusalem (2:1-10), which occurred fourteen years after his meeting with Peter. During this visit Paul explained to the church at Jerusalem the circumcision-free gospel he preached among the Gentiles, and he defended "the truth of the gospel" (2:5) against certain "false brothers" (2:4) who would have compelled his Gentile converts to be circumcised. Sometime after this visit, a second episode occurred at Antioch (2:11-15) where Jewish and Gentile Christians were sharing table fellowship, even though Jewish Law forbade Jews to eat with Gentiles who did not obey the dietary prescriptions of the Law. When certain Jewish believers associated with James came to Antioch, therefore, they forced Peter, Barnabas, and other Jewish Christians to withdraw from table fellowship with Gentiles. It was at this point that Paul reprimanded Peter for no longer being in line with "the truth of the gospel" (2:14).

The truth of gospel affirms that a person is not justified on the basis of doing the works of the Jewish Law such as its dietary prescriptions but on the basis of what God has done in Christ. This is why Gentiles and Jewish believers have put their faith in Christ rather than rely on the works of the Law.

The works of the Law include all of the prescriptions of the Mosaic law, ritual as well as moral. But as the context of Galatians shows, Paul is especially concerned about those prescriptions that outwardly identify one as Jewish, for example, the Law's dietary prescriptions. His thought can be paraphrased in this manner:

> God does not acquit or rectify us because of legal observance of those laws that outwardly identify one as Jewish: circumcision, dietary prescriptions, Sabbath observance. If justification came through legal observance, there would have been no need for God to send his Son to justify us. That God sent his Son indicates that it was not the purpose of the Law to effect justification. Justification comes from what God accomplished in Christ. This is why we entrust ourselves to Christ rather than rely on the works of Law. It is God who declares that we are innocent. I was

the most zealous of Jews, but I have set aside my zeal for the law which, by a strange twist of irony, brought me to the moment of my call and conversion.

Paul's teaching on justification was the point of contention between Protestants and Catholics at the time of the Reformation. While Lutherans and Catholics have come to substantial agreement on this point today, many Catholics are still puzzled by the language of justification. This text provides preachers with an opportunity to summarize the essential points of Paul's teaching. For, even though Paul's situation was different from ours, the essential point remains the same: God justifies us through his Son, Jesus Christ. We do not "earn" our salvation nor can we justify ourselves in God's sight. Sinners that we are, we depend on the graciousness of God.

One in Christ
Twelfth Sunday: Gal 3:26-29

This week's reading is the conclusion to a rather long and intricate argument which Paul develops in chapter 3 to dissuade the Galatians from having themselves circumcised and adopting a Jewish way of life. The argument proceeds in this way.

In 3:1-6 Paul asks the Galatians a series of rhetorical questions about their experience of the Spirit. When and how did they receive the Spirit? By doing the works of the Law, or by trusting faith in the message of the crucified Christ that Paul preached to them? Since the Galatians had not yet begun to do the works of the Law, the answer to Paul's question is clear. They received the Spirit by believing in the message of the gospel, not by doing the works of the Law. Since the experience of the Spirit is the assurance of their justification, there is no need for the Galatians to adopt a Jewish way of life by doing the works of the Law.

Next (3:7-14), Paul draws a distinction between two kinds of people: those who stand under the threatening curse of the Law pronounced in Deuteronomy, and those who enjoy the blessing of the Spirit which God promised to faithful Abraham. Paul argues that if the Galatians put themselves under the Law they will also put themselves under the Law's threatening curse from which Christ freed them by dying on the cross. But if they follow the example of faithful Abraham, they will enjoy the promised blessing of the Spirit.

Having reminded the Galatians that they enjoy God's Spirit apart from doing the works of the Law, Paul shows them that they are already Abraham's children, apart from circumcision. The argument here is rather complicated and need not be part of any sermon, but it is important for preachers to be aware of it. According to Paul's reading of Genesis, the promises God made to Abraham envisioned a singular descendant: the Christ. The Mosaic Law, which came after the promises were made, did not alter the promises God made to Abraham's descendant, the Christ, or the condition on which they depended, faith. Consequently, those who are in Christ are Abraham's descendants. More specifically, the Galatians are Abraham's descendants because they have been incorporated into Christ through baptism. There is no need, then, for them to have themselves circumcised and adopt a Jewish way of life by doing the works of the Law.

Then why did God give the Law? The Law had a temporary role in salvation history. In the period between the promise and its fulfillment, the Law was humanity's disciplinarian. That is, it showed humanity what God required, though it did not give humanity the power to do what it required. Now that Christ has come, the Law has fulfilled its role in salvation history. There is no need to put oneself under its regime. What God requires is trusting faith in Jesus Christ.

The argument I have summarized does not belong in the Sunday homily, but it is important for preachers to understand the movement of Paul's thought if they hope to make sense of this text. In effect, Paul says that Christ has broken down the barriers that separate people from each other: race, social status, gender. While these external differences remain, they do not affect our status before God. God justifies people on the basis of what he has done in his Son. Thus, there is a radical equality in Christ that overcomes every barrier of gender, class, or race. At a time when class, race, and gender remain causes of painful division and strife, those who preach from this text might proclaim the social dimension of Paul's teaching on justification by faith.

Freedom, Responsibility, and the Spirit
Thirteenth Sunday: Gal 5:1, 13-18

Thus far, the Lectionary readings have focused on justification by faith apart from doing the works of the Law. However, if believers are no longer under the Law, how can they live a moral life? Does not Paul's teaching subvert the moral life by providing a license for believers to do whatever they want? Aware that his teaching is liable to misinterpretation, Paul takes up the question of the moral life in the final chapters of Galatians.

His argument can be summarized as follows. Although the justified are no longer under the Law, they *fulfill* the Law through the love commandment thanks to the presence of God's Spirit. This Spirit produces its fruit within them: "love, joy, peace, patience, kindness, generosity, faithfulness, gentleness, self-control" (5:23). Opposed to this Spirit is the power of the flesh, which Paul understands as a moral force that produces works of immorality and dissension which destroy the fabric of community life (see 5:19-21). Accordingly, Paul encourages his converts to live by the Spirit (5:16), be guided by the Spirit (5:18), and follow the Spirit (5:25). If they do, the Spirit will produce its fruit within them, and they will fulfill the law of Christ (6:2). They will live the Law as Christ did, in light of the love commandment.

Justification by faith results in good deeds, and Paul does not hesitate to say, "Let us not grow tired of doing good" (6:9). The justified are free, but their freedom is not license. Aware that the power of the flesh is close at hand, he warns his converts not to let their freedom become an opportunity for the power of the flesh to take advantage of them. Freed from the Law, they are to enslave themselves to each other in love. The antidote to the flesh is the power of the Spirit which enables the justified to do God's will.

Catholics have always been somewhat uncomfortable with Paul's teaching on justification by faith apart from works. It sounds so very Lutheran! A careful reading of Galatians 5–6 should assure even the most skeptical that there is nothing to fear. Paul expects the justified to live a moral life, and he is confident that they can do so when guided by the Spirit.

This text provides preachers with a marvelous opportunity to discuss the Spirit and the moral life. Preachers might contrast two ways of life: one under the power of the flesh, the other led by the power of God's Spirit. The first way focuses on the self and produces works that lead to community dissension. It is a life in servitude to sin, and its wages are death. The second way is a life of freedom to serve others in love. Its power comes from the Spirit which produces its fruit in believers. Those who allow themselves to be guided by this Spirit will fulfill the law of Christ.

The Cross of Christ and the New Creation
Fourteenth Week: Gal 6:14-18

The final reading of Galatians is part of the letter's conclusion (6:11-18) in which Paul summarizes the main points he has made throughout the letter. Once again, then, preachers should read the text within its context if they wish to appreciate its full meaning.

To this point Paul has used a secretary, but because his concluding remarks are so important, he writes the final portion of this letter in his own hand, and with large letters. Having pointed this out (6:11), he calls into question the motivation and sincerity of those who would compel the Galatians to be circumcised (6:12-14). They are trying to avoid being persecuted for the cross of Christ, he says. Moreover, not even they do all of the works of the Law. While they boast in the outward sign of circumcision, Paul boasts in the cross of Christ through which he has been crucified to the world and the world to him. That is to say, he has died to the world of sin, so that sin is no longer alive for him. Consequently, Paul lives in and for a new creation in which circumcision, or the lack of it, has become a matter of indifference as far as salvation is concerned. Those who live according to this new creation live by "this rule" (6:15); that is, God's new creation in Christ. Circumcised or not, such people belong "to the Israel of God" (6:16), a people of God's own choosing. Paul himself belongs to this new creation, and he has the scars and marks of persecution to prove it.

These final remarks summarize the major theme of Galatians; namely, for those who have been justified in Christ, there is no distinction between Gentile and Jew since for both God has effected a new creation in Christ. Those who preach from this text, then, might consider focusing on the theme of the new creation that God continually effects in Christ, even in our own day. This new creation is a people, "the Israel of God," who have embraced the cross of Christ. In doing so, they have died to the world of sin and illusion so that they might live for God and Christ. Apart from such daily crucifixion, there is no death to the world; there is no new creation.

Strategy: Theological Themes

Those who preach from Galatians will find themselves dealing with Paul's teaching on justification. It may be helpful, therefore, to provide some background about this teaching.

The language of justification comes from the secular law court where a judge acquits or condemns a defendant. When acquitting a defendant, the judge proclaims that the defendant is innocent because the defendant stands in the proper relationship to the Law. The defendant is "justified" in the sight of the Law. When this language is transferred to the religious sphere, the judge is God, the defendant is the human person, and the law is God's law. Pious Israelites, who observed the precepts of the Law, stood in the proper covenant relationship to God, and they trusted that God would justify or acquit them at the final judgment.

Before his call, Paul sought to be justified or acquitted by such legal observance. In his Letter to the Philippians he writes, "In zeal I persecuted the church, in righteousness based on the law I was blameless" (Phil 3:6). When God revealed his Son to Paul, however, he realized that the righteousness he had attained by legal observance was of no account: "whatever gains I had, these I have come to consider a loss because of Christ" (Phil 3:7).

Paul now understood that the righteousness that is pleasing to God does not come from legal observance, otherwise "Christ died for nothing" (Gal 2:21). That Christ died for sins indicates that he did something which the Law could not. Paul now viewed Christ as his righteousness (1 Cor 1:30), the source of his justification. He understood that God acquits a person on the basis of trusting faith rather than legal observance.

In the Reformation period the debate was about the nature of justification. While Protestants focused on the legal dimension of the metaphor, Catholics insisted on the reality of what happened: the justified are truly transformed and sanctified. Today there is substantial agreement among Catholics and Protestants about the meaning of justification. Justification is God's work, not ours. The proper response to this work is trusting faith in what God has done. This faith is accompanied by good works; and, although they will not justify the believer, such works are essential for the moral life of those who are justified by God's grace.

Colossians

The Lectionary draws from Colossians five times during the course of Year C. The use of this letter is not surprising since Colossians is especially rich in christology, ecclesiology, and teaching on the moral life. For example, the hymn-like passage of 1:15-20, which presents Christ as the image of the invisible God and the firstborn of all creation, points to the pre-existence of Christ. In that same passage and elsewhere in the letter, Colossians identifies Christ as the head of the body, which is the Church (1:18; 2:19). He is the mystery of God hidden for ages but now revealed through the preaching of Paul. This mystery, which is Christ, is the foundation of the moral life. Having been delivered from the power of darkness and transferred to the kingdom of God's beloved Son (1:13), believers have been raised up with Christ (3:1-4) and called to live a life worthy of their calling. A careful reading of Colossians will enable those who preach from it to explain the christological basis of the moral life.

Strategy: Understanding the Context

The Historical Context. The Pauline authorship of Colossians is disputed. Many contemporary scholars categorize it as deutero-Pauline, arguing that another wrote this letter in Paul's name. This issue need not concern preachers who will do best to refer to the author as Paul. For, even if Colossians was written by another in Paul's name, its teaching about Christ is thoroughly Pauline.

Paul writes from prison (4:3). The place of his imprisonment is not identified, however, since there would have been no need to inform the Colossians of what they already knew. Tychicus and Onesimus are probably the bearers of the letter (4:7-9). The community itself seems to have been established by one of Paul's co-workers, Epaphras (1:7), rather than by Paul.

Paul's purpose is twofold. On the one hand, he writes to warn the Colossians of certain teachers who were encouraging them to adopt ascetic practices, either to appease angelic powers or to enjoy a vision of them (2:4-23). In response to this teaching, Paul insists that the fullness of the deity dwells bodily in Christ who has conquered the principalities and powers. Consequently, there is no need to appease or seek visions of these angelic powers through ascetical practices. What God has done in Christ is sufficient for salvation.

In addition to warning the Colossians of being seduced by such teaching, Paul uses the occasion of this letter to provide them with an extended moral exhortation. This exhortation depends on, and flows from, Paul's christology: believers must seek what is above because they have been raised up with Christ. Having died with him, they must put to death all that is evil. Colossians, then, provides a marvelous example of how the moral life of believers is rooted in the salvation they already experience in Christ.

The Literary Context. The literary structure of Colossians corresponds to Paul's twofold concern. In the opening chapters he focuses on the preeminence of Christ and the danger posed by teachers who would entice the Colossians to adopt an ascetic way of life. In the final chapters of the letter, he exhorts the

Colossians to adopt a moral life which corresponds to their new life in Christ. The letter may be summarized in this way.

- A.   Paul greets the Colossians and gives thanks for what God has done for them in Christ: God has delivered them from the power of darkness and transferred them into the kingdom of his beloved Son (1:1-14).
- B.   Paul extols the preeminence of Christ (1:15–2:23).
  1.   Christ is the agent of God's creation and reconciliation (1:15-20).
  2.   Paul's sufferings play a role in God's plan (1:21–2:3).
  3.   The Colossians should beware of teachers whose ascetical practices devalue what God has done in Christ (2:4-23).
- C.   Those who have been raised up in Christ ought to live a moral life (3:1–4:6).
  1.   The moral life is based on Christ's death and resurrection (3:1-4).
  2.   Therefore, the Colossians ought to put to death all vices and put on virtue (3:5-17).
  3.   Members of the household should be subject to their superiors (3:18–4:1).
  4.   The Colossians must persevere in prayer (4:2-6).
- D.   Paul and his co-workers greet the Colossians (4:7-18).

Strategy: The Text in Context

Christ's Role in Creation and Redemption
Fifteenth Sunday: Col 1:15-20

This passage is also used on the Feast of Christ the King. On that occasion, however, the Lectionary begins the reading at 1:12 rather than 1:15. This decision makes eminent sense for the Feast of Christ the King since vv. 13-14 refer to the kingdom of the Son, the focus of this feast: "He [God] delivered us from the power of darkness and transferred us to the kingdom of his beloved Son, in whom we have redemption, for the forgiveness of sins." Those who choose to preach from 1:15-20 should keep vv. 13-14 in view since they are the immediate introduction to this week's reading which celebrates Christ's role in creation and redemption. Preachers should also pay attention to the verses that immediately follow this passage (1:21-23) since they suggest a story of past alienation and present reconciliation which this passage presupposes.

Many have suggested that Col 1:15-20 was a liturgical hymn that Paul incorporated into this letter to remind the Colossians of Christ's surpassing dignity. Whether or not it was, it is clearly a poetic piece that can be divided into two parts. In the first (1:15-18a) Paul celebrates Christ's role in the order of creation, and in the second he recalls Christ's work in the order of redemption (1:18b-20).

As regards Christ's role in creation, Paul insists that all things were created *in, through,* and *for* Christ who is the very image of the invisible God and the firstborn of all creation. All things here includes those in heaven as well as those on earth, what cannot be seen as well as what can be seen. Everything, even the angelic beings which the Colossians may have been tempted to worship, was created in, through, and for Christ. The reason for this is related to Christ's identity: he is the image of the God who cannot be seen; he is the firstborn of all creation. By identifying him as the image of the invisible God, Paul says that Christ is the perfect representation of God. He writes in 2:9, "For in him dwells the whole fullness of the deity bodily." By calling Christ the "firstborn of all creation," Paul affirms the preeminence of Christ since all things were created in, through, and for him. In effect, Paul points to the pre-existence of Christ.

Paul concludes the first part of this passage by identifying Christ as "the head of the body, the church." By affirming that Christ is the head of the body and that the body is the Church, Colossians and Ephesians develop the notion of the Church as the body of Christ in a slightly different way than do Rom 12:3-8 and 1 Cor 12:12-31. Whereas Romans and 1 Corinthians employ this image in a functional way (the body has many parts and each plays a role), Colossians and Ephesians use the image in a more figurative manner: Christ is the head of the body which *is* the Church. Accordingly, Colossians and Ephesians view the Church as the universal Church rather than as the local community, as Romans and 1 Corinthians do. In doing so, Colossians and Ephesians open the door for a christology which is cosmic in scope.

Having established the preeminence of Christ in the order of creation and announced that he is the head of the Church, in the second part of this passage Paul turns to Christ's role in the order of redemption. Echoing the language of the first part of the hymn, where he identified Christ as "the firstborn of all creation," he calls Christ "the firstborn from the dead," clearly referring to the resurrection which established the preeminence of Christ in the order of redemption. Then, affirming that "the fullness" was pleased to dwell *in* Christ, Paul says that *all things* were reconciled *through* him and *for him.* Consequently, all things, *whether on earth or in heaven* have been reconciled by the blood of Christ's cross.

As the italicized words show, there is a parallelism between Christ's role in the order of creation and in the order of redemption. Just as all things in heaven and on earth were created in, through, and for him, so all things in heaven and on earth were reconciled through and for him in whom "the fullness was pleased to dwell." This fullness is the very being of God (see 2:9).

At a time when the news media is filled with stories about the Jesus of history, some of which are sensational in nature, this text challenges preachers to say something about Christ and his work. Who is the one in whose name we gather each week to celebrate the Eucharist? What has he done that we still remember him two thousand years later? To be sure, he was a prophetic figure and an extraordinary religious teacher. More than a prophetic and religious figure, however, he is the pre-existent one in whom, through whom, and for whom God created all things. His death effected a reconciliation that is cosmic in scope and which could not have been accomplished apart from the shedding of his blood. The Church does not gather week after week to remember a figure of the past but to celebrate its creation and redemption in, through, and by the one who is the very image of the unseen God, the one in whom the fullness of deity dwells.

The Sufferings of Paul and the Mystery of God
Sixteenth Sunday: Col 1:24-28

Having celebrated the role of Christ in creation and redemption, Paul speaks of his ministerial role and the sufferings
he endures for the sake of the body which is the Church. The
text is part of a larger unit that consists of 1:21–2:3, and preachers will do well to reflect on this reading in light of that unit.

At the beginning of the unit (1:21), Paul contrasts the former situation of the Colossians with their present status in
Christ. *Once* they were alienated from God, *now* they have been
reconciled through Christ's death so that Christ might present
them to God blameless and irreproachable. Paul is the minister
of this gospel of reconciliation.

Although this gospel entails great suffering for Paul, he rejoices in his suffering because it is beneficial to the Colossians
and those to whom he preaches the good news. As Paul sees it,
he is "filling up what is lacking in the afflictions of Christ on behalf of his body, which is the church" (1:24). This phrase is puzzling because it seems to imply that there was something lacking
in the sufferings of Christ that Paul must supplement through his
ministry. This is not what Paul is saying. By "the afflictions of
Christ," he means the messianic sufferings that the Church must
endure before the end. These afflictions are the sufferings that
the Church endures as a consequence of its witness to Christ.
Deeply aware of this, Paul rejoices in his apostolic suffering because it is for the sake of the Church, the body of Christ.

As Christ's minister, Paul has been entrusted with "the
mystery of God" (2:2). This mystery was hidden for ages, but it
has now been revealed to God's holy ones, among whom are
the Colossians. The mystery *is* Christ who dwells in the Colossians and all Gentiles who have believed in the gospel.

The goal of Paul's ministry is to "present everyone perfect
in Christ" (1:28). The meaning of the Greek word *teleios* is "complete" or "whole." Thus the purpose of Paul's ministry is to bring
his converts to the final purpose and goal of their lives which is
to stand "holy, without blemish, and irreproachable" before God
(1:22). This perfection will be attained when the entire body is

perfectly united with its head, who is Christ, "from whom the whole body, supported and held together by its ligaments and bonds, achieves the growth that comes from God" (2:19). Put another way, the destiny of the believer is intimately connected with the destiny of the body that is the Church. Apart from that body, individuals cannot attain their final goal.

Although this text focuses on Paul's apostolic ministry, it is closely related to last week's reading, which dealt with the person and work of Christ. The mystery of God, of which Paul is a minister, is Christ in, through, and for whom God created and reconciled the world. Hidden for ages, this mystery has been revealed in Christ who now dwells in those who believe. Those who preach from this text will do well to focus on this mystery, especially as it is expressed in the words, "It is Christ in you, the hope for glory" (1:27). This phrase summarizes the whole purpose of God's plan: that Christ dwell in believers so that they may participate in the very glory of God. As the image of the unseen God and the firstborn from the dead, he embodies the destiny of humanity. That destiny cannot be attained apart from the Church which is his body. The mystery of God, then, is the intimate relationship between Christ and believers that finds its sacramental expression in the Eucharist.

Buried and Raised with Christ
Seventeenth Sunday: Col 2:12-14

This text occurs in the middle of a unit in which Paul warns the Colossians not to be led astray by any teaching that encourages them to adopt an ascetical way of life in order to appease, or attain a vision of, angelic beings (2:4-23). Although the worshipping assembly will not be aware of this background, those who preach from this text should be.

Paul begins by admonishing the Colossians not to be led astray by any teaching that is based on the "elemental powers of the world" (2:8) rather than on Christ (1:4-8). By this enigmatic phrase, Paul may be referring to angelic beings such as the principalities and powers mentioned in v. 15. Such a teaching would have placed Christ in a subordinate role to the elemental powers of the world.

Having warned the Colossians not to be seduced by such teaching, Paul reminds them of Christ's person and work (2:9-15). He notes that the fullness of divinity dwells in him, and Christ has authority over every angelic being. The Colossians were circumcised with "the circumcision of Christ" (2:11) when they were buried and raised with him in their baptism. In that baptism they shared in Christ's victory on the cross where he conquered "the principalities and the powers" (2:15), the very beings the Colossians may have been tempted to appease.

Having reminded the Colossians of Christ's work on their behalf, Paul warns them not to adopt the ascetical practices that some are urging (2:16-23). Exactly what Paul is referring to is not clear. Some suggest that certain people were promoting such practices as a way of appeasing the elemental powers of the world. Whatever the problem, Paul's admonition is clear. There is no need to submit to these practices because the Colossians have died with Christ "to the elemental powers of the world" (2:20).

In limiting itself to vv. 12-14, the Lectionary intends to draw attention to the theme of baptism as a process of being buried and raised up with Christ. The context of this reading, however, shows how Paul views baptism in light of Christ's redemptive work. Baptism is a participation in Christ's death on the cross which was a cosmic victory over every power, heavenly as well as earthly. Those who are baptized into Christ participate in his cosmic victory of reconciliation.

This text provides preachers with an opportunity to present baptism from a slightly different perspective: Christ's cosmic victory. Seen from this perspective, baptism is more than a rite of initiation. It is participation in a victory over every power that sets itself against God. Through baptism, believers are so closely associated with Christ's victory that they are buried and raised up with him. Consequently, if they hold fast to Christ they need not do something above and beyond what God has accomplished in Christ.

The Moral Life of Believers
Eighteenth Sunday: Col 3:1-5, 9-11

Whereas the first three readings from Colossians were drawn from that part of the letter which focuses on the person and work of Christ, this reading comes from that part of the letter which exhorts the Colossians to live a life that conforms with what Christ has done for them (3:1–4:6). In this regard Colossians is a marvelous example of how Paul's moral exhortation depends on his doctrinal exposition: believers are to live in a particular way because Christ has reconciled them to God through his saving death.

In the first two verses of this reading, Paul presents the fundamental principle of the moral life for those who believe in Christ: if they have been raised up with him, then they should seek what is above. They are no longer to think of earthly things because, in baptism, they have died with Christ. At the present time their life is hidden in Christ, but when Christ returns in glory, their glory will be revealed. The basic principle is to live in accordance with one's new being.

Having established this principle, Paul exhorts the Colossians to put to death inappropriate behavior such as immorality, so that they may put on the new self that is being renewed in the image of God. Remembering that Christ is the image of God (1:15), they must live as people who are being renewed in God's image. Those who are being renewed in this image belong to a new humanity in which the barriers of race and social class have been broken down because "Christ is all and in all" (3:11).

This text provides an opportunity to talk about the moral life. Why do we live the way we do? What is the purpose and goal of our lives? Paul's response is clear: Christians live in a way that corresponds to their new life in Christ. Having been raised up with Christ, they seek to embrace the new self that he has obtained for them through his saving death and resurrection. The structure of the moral life, then, begins with the indicative of salvation before moving to the moral imperative. Rather than tell people what to do, Paul reminds them of their new life in Christ and exhorts them to live accordingly. This is the proper model for moral instruction.

Strategy: Theology Themes

Three themes dominate the letter to the Colossians: the primacy of Christ, the scope of his redemptive work, and the implications of that work for the moral life. Since the first two themes are most fully developed in 1:15-20, preachers should reflect on that passage even if they do not choose to preach from it, for its themes occur throughout the letter.

When preaching about the primacy of Christ the focus will be on the mystery of God, which Paul identifies as Christ. Before creation, Christ was with God, and when all things were created, they were created in, through, and for Christ. As the head of the body, the Church, Christ now lives in believers.

When preaching about the work of Christ, the focus will be on his work of reconciliation which is cosmic in scope. All things have been reconciled through and for Christ who has overcome every hostile power. By the blood of his cross, he has reconciled everything, in heaven and on earth, and there is nothing to fear.

Finally, preaching about the moral life must be related to the primacy and work of Christ. Any other kind of preaching is mere moralism because it gives people a list of dos and don'ts without explaining the inner motivation for living a moral life.

Hebrews

During Year C the Lectionary, which has already made extensive use of Hebrews in Year B, draws upon this writing four more times. However, whereas the readings from Year B focused on the theme of the high priesthood of Christ, those of Year C come from a section of Hebrews that summons readers to faithful endurance because they have such a high priest.

As I noted in my earlier discussion of Hebrews, Paul was not the author of this writing. But since there was a strong tradition in the early Church of the East that he was its author, and since many of its themes are similar to those found in Paul's letters, I include Hebrews in my discussion of preaching from Paul. Since I have already discussed the background to Hebrews in Year B, I refer readers to that discussion.

Strategy: Understanding the Context

The Literary Context. The readings from Hebrews during Year C come from two extensive moral exhortations (10:26–12:13; 12:14–13:19) which presuppose the doctrinal exposition of the high priesthood of Christ that is found in the earlier sections of the letter, especially the great central section (5:11–10:25). The first of these exhortations is a call to faithful endurance (10:26–12:13) and will be familiar to many because of chapter 11, which recounts outstanding examples of faith from Israel's past. Three of the readings from Hebrews (Heb 11:1-2, 8-19; 12:1-4; 12:5-7, 11-13) are taken from this section.

The section begins with a preparatory exhortation that consists of two parts (10:26-39). In the first (10:26-31) Hebrews sternly warns its audience that there is no further sacrifice for sins beyond what Christ has accomplished. Therefore, it is imperative that believers respond positively to the salvation offered in Christ. In the second (10:32-39), Hebrews recalls its audience's heroic behavior in the past when it endured "a great contest of suffering" (10:32). Quoting from the prophet Habakkuk (2:4), it reminds its audience that those who are just will live by faith and then concludes, "We are not among those who draw back and perish, but among those who have faith and will possess life" (10:39).

The quotation from Habakkuk and the affirmation that the audience consists of those who have faith announces the theme of chapter 11, the power of faith. Beginning with creation and moving through Israel's history from Abel to the Maccabees, Hebrews recounts example after example of men and women who lived by faith. The chapter can be outlined as follows:

11:1-2	An introduction in which Hebrews explains what faith is.
11:3-7	Four examples of faith: knowledge of the creation of the universe by faith, the faith of Abel, Enoch, and Noah.
11:8-12	The faith of Abraham: his call, his sojourn, the birth of Isaac.

11:13-16   A reflection on the faith of those who died without attaining the promise but greeted it from afar confident of a better homeland.

11:17-22   A resumption of the story and faith of Abraham: his willingness to sacrifice Isaac; Isaac's blessing of Jacob and Esau; Jacob's blessing of his sons; Jacob's instructions to retrieve his bones from Egypt.

11:23-31   The example of Moses and the generation of the Exodus: the faith of Moses' parents; Moses' faith in leaving Pharaoh's court and Egypt; Moses' faith in keeping the Passover; the crossing of the Red Sea; the fall of Jericho and the faith of Rahab.

11:32-40   The faith of other men and women whom the author does not name but who hoped "to obtain a better resurrection" (11:35).

As preachers reflect on this chapter, they will note the repeated use of the phrase "By faith" that occurs eighteen times in vv. 3-31. Such repetition reminds readers of the definition of faith in 11:1 and reinforces the quotation from Habakkuk that the just shall live by faith.

Having presented this "cloud of witnesses" from Israel's past (12:1), Hebrews calls its audience to faithful endurance (12:1-13). To do so, it exhorts the audience to keep its eyes fixed on Jesus "the leader and perfecter of faith" (12:2). Then, quoting Prov 3:11-12, it reminds its hearers that the Lord disciplines those whom he loves (12:4-6). In light of this maxim, Hebrews exhorts its listeners to endure their trials as discipline from God, just as they submit to and learn from the discipline administered by their earthly fathers (12:7-11). Finally, Hebrews calls its audience to strengthen itself for the race that lies ahead (12:12-13).

The second and last exhortation consists of 12:14–13:19 and can be outlined as follows:

12:14-17   A warning against failure.

12:18-39   The new situation of believers.

12:18-24   The city of the living God, the heavenly Jeru-
            salem.
12:25-30   The unshakeable kingdom.
13:1-19   Community life and the new sacrifice.

The fourth reading from Hebrews (12:18-19, 22-24a)
comes from this section and, as the outline shows, it deals with
the new situation in which believers find themselves. Unlike Israel of old, which stood before the fearsome sight of Mount
Sinai, the new community of faith has approached the city of
the living God thanks to the blood of Jesus, who is "the mediator of a new covenant" (12:24). Consequently, they have every
confidence to endure in their time of suffering because, like the
cloud of witnesses described in chapter 11, they know the good
things that lie before them.

The Text in Its Context

The Faith by Which We Live
Nineteenth Sunday: Heb 11:1-2, 8-19

This is the only Lectionary reading from chapter 11, and it
may well be the most important of the four readings from Hebrews since it provides the definition of faith that undergirds
everything that follows. Therefore, preachers will do well to reflect on this definition in light of chapter 11 since they will find
themselves returning to this concept again and again.

As the outline shows, the chapter and this reading begin
with a definition of faith that the New American Bible translates
in this way: "Faith is the realization of what is hoped for and evidence of things not seen" (11:1). The definition is twofold.
First, faith is the support for what we hope for; second, it provides the evidence for those things that people do not see and
yet know exist. Since every translation is already an interpretation, it is helpful to consult other translations:

Now faith is the substance of things hoped for, the evidence
of things not seen (*The King James Version*).

Now faith is the substance of things to be hoped for, the evidence of things that appear not (*The Rheims New Testament*).

What is faith? It is that which gives substance to our hopes, which convinces us of things we cannot see (*R.A. Knox Translation*).

Faith is the foundation of the blessings for which we hope, the proof of the realities which we do not see (*J.A. Kleist & J. Lilly Translation*).

Now faith means putting our full confidence in the things we hope for; it means being certain of things we cannot see (*J.B. Phillips Translation*).

Now faith is being sure of what we hope for and certain of what we do not see (*New International Version*).

Now faith is the assurance of things hoped for, the conviction of things not seen (*New Revised Standard Version*).

Faith gives substance to our hopes and convinces us of realities we do not see (*Revised New English Bible*).

These translations suggest that the most difficult part of the text is the first, which the NAB translates, "Faith is the realization of what is hoped for." In this translation the NAB appears to equate faith with the realization of hope. In my view, the translations of the NRSV and the RNEB are more helpful: Faith undergirds what we hope for because it provides assurance or gives substance to what we hope for. For example, Abraham obeyed God's call and sojourned in a foreign land *because* faith assured him that he would eventually come to the city "whose architect and maker is God" (11:10).

The meaning of the second part of the definition is easier to comprehend. Faith provides the evidence for what we cannot see. That is, faith allows us to see what those without faith cannot. Noah acted with this faith when he built the ark, even though the flood had not yet begun. It is this faith which helps one to understand that God created the universe, even though no one saw the act of creation. To summarize, Hebrews uses faith in a slightly different way than those writings of the New Testament which speak of trusting faith in Christ or God. For

Hebrews faith is more akin to knowledge or understanding, inasmuch as it provides assurance and proof of what lies ahead, even though it cannot be seen. As preachers reflect on the examples of faith in this text, they should keep this definition in mind.

Although chapter 11 presents the examples of several men and women who exhibited faith, the Lectionary focuses on Abraham. The phrase "By faith" occurs four times, thereby indicating four examples of Abraham's faith: (1) he obeyed when called; (2) he sojourned in the promised land as in a foreign country; (3) he received the power to generate even though he was of an advanced age; and (4) he offered Isaac when put to the test. In each instance, Abraham acted because faith assured him of something better. Thus, he obeyed God's call because he knew he would receive an inheritance. He sojourned in the promised land because he was looking for the lasting city. He received the power to generate because he believed in the power of the God who made the promise. And he was willing to offer his only son because he reasoned that God could raise the dead. In other words, faith supported what he hoped for and assured him that he would not be disappointed. Faith was the proof for what he could not see.

Between the third and fourth examples of faith, Hebrews recalls those who died in faith. Like Abraham, they viewed themselves as "strangers and aliens" (11:13) who were seeking a better homeland. Though they could not see the heavenly city, faith assured them that they would inherit it, even if they died before the promise was attained. Thus Hebrews affirms that God is the God whose promises are faithfully fulfilled, even when death says that there is no reason to believe.

Everybody believes in something, even if they believe in the nothingness and emptiness of life. What or who we believe in, however, makes the difference. Who or what we believe in determines how we live. For example, those who believe and hope in their career or financial security will live in a way that corresponds with such faith, while those who believe in something that transcends what they see and apprehend with their senses will live in another way. Abraham exemplified the kind of faith that sought what he could not see. Searching for a heavenly city, he was content to live as a foreigner in a land his descendants would inherit.

This text affords preachers an opportunity to reflect on the kind of faith that makes ordinary people extraordinary. Hebrews challenges preachers to imitate its own powerful rhetoric in order to persuade their congregations to live by faith.

The Faith of Jesus
Twentieth Sunday: Heb 12:1-4

In chapter 11 Hebrews provided numerous examples of faith from Israel's history: examples of people who acted on the basis of a better hope even though they did not attain the goal for which they hoped while they were alive. On the basis of these examples, Hebrews appeals to its audience to embrace a similar life of faith since it is surrounded by "so great a cloud of witnesses" (12:1). This cloud of witnesses consists of the men and women of old who have attained faith's goal. Like runners in a marathon, they are witnesses to others that the race can be run. And like spectators in a stadium, they wait for those still running to complete the race so that they may crown them with the victor's wreath.

In addition to this cloud of witnesses, Hebrews celebrates Jesus, "the leader and perfecter of faith." He is the leader of our faith because he is the source of faith, the first to have attained the ultimate goal of faith. Thus, he now sits "at the right of the throne of God" (12:2). He is the perfecter of faith because he perfectly embodies faith. In him faith and fidelity are brought to fulfillment. Like a long-distance runner who endures the pain and effort of the race because he is looking to the finish line, Jesus endured the shame of the cross for the sake of the heavenly glory that awaited him. Reminding its audience that it has not yet had to shed its blood in the struggle against sin, Hebrews exhorts its listeners to imitate the faith of this great crowd of witnesses, especially the faith of Jesus.

Christians believe in and trust in Jesus, but they seldom think of him as a man of faith. This is not surprising since Christians often think of faith in terms of creeds. In identifying Jesus as the leader and perfecter of faith, however, Hebrews is quite insistent that Jesus, like the crowd of witnesses that preceded him, was sustained by faith. Those who preach from this text have an opportunity to introduce their congregations to an aspect of Jesus' humanity that is too seldom discussed: the faith of Jesus. This faith is the faithfulness of Jesus who trusted that God would vindicate him despite the shame of the cross.

Learning Discipline
Twenty-first Sunday: Heb 12:5-7, 11-13

This reading brings the moral exhortation of 10:26–12:13 to a close. Having presented its audience with a cloud of faithful witnesses, Hebrews calls its listeners to faithful endurance. The text revolves around Prov 3:11-12: the Lord disciplines those whom he loves. Reminding its audience that even their earthly fathers disciplined them, Hebrews exhorts its listeners to endure their trials as discipline from the heavenly Father.

Although it is not explicitly developed here, Hebrews is drawing a lesson from the life of Jesus who, "Son though he was, he learned obedience from what he suffered; and when he was made perfect, he became the source of eternal salvation for all who obey him" (5:8). Hebrews views the present sufferings of believers as a form of divine discipline that is ultimately meant to bring forth a harvest of good behavior ("righteousness").

Having made this point, Hebrews returns to the athletic imagery so prominent in last week's reading. Its audience is to stand up straight despite its present affliction and finish the race it has begun.

An exhortation such as this is best preached in light of the context that prepares for it. Preachers would do well, then, to plan their preaching so that they can determine what texts of Hebrews they will focus on. If they decide to deal with this text, their preaching will be most effective if they relate it to the faith of Jesus and to the faith of the cloud of witnesses in chapter 11. In doing so, preachers might make the point that authentic faith involves suffering and trial. Thus Jesus, when he was about to

die, "offered prayers and supplications with loud cries and tears
to the one who was able to save him from death" (Heb 5:7).

The City of the Living God
Twenty-second Sunday: Heb 12:18-19, 22-24a

This text occurs at the beginning of the final exhortation of
Hebrews (12:14–13:19). Accordingly, preachers will need to
read it within this context if they wish to appreciate its full
meaning.

Immediately before this week's text, Hebrews gives the third
of its harsh warnings (12:14-17; the other two are 5:11–6:20 and
10:26-39). In this warning, Hebrews recalls the story of Esau who
surrendered his birthright to his father's blessing for a bowl of
porridge and was unable to receive it back. The lesson is clear: if
the audience of Hebrews falters now there will be no opportunity
to turn back later. Consequently, believers must persevere all the
more.

After this harsh warning, Hebrews returns to a theme that
it introduced earlier: a comparison between the wilderness generation that failed to remain faithful and the new community
that must live by faith (see 3:7–4:11). Unlike that generation
which approached the fearsome sight of Mount Sinai, the new
generation has approached "the city of the living God, the heavenly Jerusalem" (12:22). Consequently, there is every reason for
confidence since the mediator of the new covenant is Jesus
whose blood is more precious than the blood of Abel of old.

In the unit that follows this week's reading (12:25-29), Hebrews exhorts its audience not to reject the one who has spoken,
namely, God. For, if Israel of old did not escape punishment, it
is all the more certain that they will not. It is within this unit that
Hebrews introduces the notion of "the unshakeable kingdom"
(12:28), yet another image for the city of the living God.

This reading provides preachers with an opportunity to
discuss the ultimate goal of the Christian life: communion with
God. Hebrews expresses this concept with numerous images:
the city of the living God, the heavenly Jerusalem, the unshakeable kingdom. In a time when many preachers shy away from

eschatological themes such as the parousia, heaven, hell, and judgment, this text challenges them to reflect on the destiny of the Christian life and find a credible way to present it to contemporary believers.

Strategy: Theological Themes

Hebrews develops two closely related themes during Year C: faith and endurance. In presenting them, it offers examples of people who endured trials for the sake of the heavenly city they could not see but, by faith, were assured of inheriting. At the head of this cloud of witnesses stands Jesus, the faithful high priest, who endured the shame of the cross for the sake of the glory that lay before him.

Although few American Christians find themselves enduring persecution of the kind presupposed in Hebrews, the need for endurance and perseverance in the Christian life remains. Indeed, the situation might be even more critical for contemporary believers, many of whom have become too settled in the earthly city and no longer look to the heavenly city whose architect is God. Hebrews is a powerful reminder that the Church is a pilgrim people who are sojourners in a foreign land. If the pilgrim people of God is to reach the unshakeable kingdom, it must live by faith as did the saints of old. Such faith makes endurance possible.

Philemon

Paul's Letter to Philemon is a mere twenty-five verses, and it only occurs once in the Lectionary. Since the Lectionary reading only reproduces vv. 9-10, 12-17, it is important for preachers to read the entire letter carefully.

Strategy: Understanding the Context

The background to this letter can be summarized in this way. Onesimus, a slave in the household of Philemon, has run away from his master and met Paul who is in prison, either in Ephesus or Rome. During this period, Onesimus became a

Christian and Paul now identifies him as his child, and himself as his father (v. 10). The slave who was once useless to his master has become useful to Paul, and a strong bond has developed between them.

This new situation, however, presents a series of problems for Onesimus, Paul, and Philemon. First, if Onesimus returns to Philemon, he will be liable to harsh and severe punishment, perhaps even death. Second, if Paul does not return Onesimus to Philemon, the bond of friendship that exists between them will be destroyed. Third, if Onesimus does return, Philemon must decide how to deal with him.

To solve this dilemma, Paul writes this letter on behalf of his new child in the faith, Onesimus, asking Philemon to receive him "no longer as a slave but more than a slave, a brother, beloved especially to me, but even more so to you, as a man and in the Lord" (v. 16). The manner in which Paul presents his request is most interesting.

First, at the outset of the letter, he greets Philemon as his co-worker (v. 1) and then reminds him of the partnership that exists between them (vv. 6, 17). Second, instead of exerting his apostolic authority and ordering Philemon to do what he wants, Paul plays on his circumstances as an old man who is in prison, and "out of love" (v. 9) he urges Philemon to do as he asks. Third, Paul says that if Onesimus has done Philemon any injustice, Philemon should charge it to Paul's account. He then adds, "May I not tell you that you owe me your very self" (v. 19).

In effect, Paul makes use of three powerful arguments: partnership in the gospel, the circumstances of his life, and the repayment of debts. First, Philemon is Paul's partner in the gospel, therefore, he should be well-disposed to Paul's request which is made in the name of the gospel. Second, Paul is not exerting his authority but acting out of love. Finally, Philemon is indebted to Paul, but Paul is willing to forgive that debt if Philemon will forgive Onesimus' debt. Thus, although this is the briefest of Paul's letters, it is a study in the power of persuasive speech.

A Man in the Lord
Twenty-third Sunday: Phil 9-10, 12-17

On first reading, Philemon seems to be a rather simple letter. Despite its appearance, it has a profound message: the gospel alters the social circumstances of those who believe in Christ. Thus, even though Onesimus probably resumed his role as Philemon's slave, the relationship between the two men could never be the same since both now belong to the same Lord. Even though Paul does not preach against the institution of slavery, he plants the seeds for its destruction when he identifies Onesimus as Philemon's brother in the Lord (v. 16).

The story of Onesimus and Philemon provides preachers with an opportunity to explain the power of the gospel that destroys barriers of race, gender, and class (see Gal 3:26). People cannot be "in the Lord" and then insist on privileges that derive from race, gender, and class without betraying the truth of the gospel. This is what Paul understood in returning Onesimus to Philemon and what Philemon had to learn when his slave returned.

1 and 2 Timothy

1 and 2 Timothy, along with Titus, are often referred to as the Pastoral Epistles because they provide Timothy and Titus with pastoral instruction for shepherding the congregations Paul entrusted to them. 1 Timothy presupposes that Paul has left Timothy in Ephesus "to instruct certain people not to teach false doctrines or concern themselves with myths and endless genealogies" (1 Tim 1:3-4). The Letter to Titus indicates that Paul has left Titus on the island of Crete so that he might "appoint presbyters in every town" (Titus 1:5), as Paul directed him.

Some question the Pauline authorship of these letters since their literary style and theological concepts often differ from that found in the non-disputed Pauline letters (Romans, 1 and 2 Corinthians, Galatians, Philippians, 1 Thessalonians, and Philemon). Moreover, it is difficult to fit the events of Paul's life, as related in these letters, into the course of his life as we know it from the Acts of the Apostles and Paul's undisputed correspondence. For these and other reasons, many Pauline scholars categorize these letters as Deutero-Pauline. While preachers should be aware of this, questions of authorship are not the concern of the homily, and preachers would be well-advised to refer to the author of these letters as Paul since this is how the canon of the New Testament understands their authorship.

Unfortunately, the Pastorals have been disparaged by some who view them as compromising Paul's teaching on justification by faith and his vibrant expectation that the parousia is at hand. Thus, some accuse the Pastorals of accommodating the gospel to a comfortable middle-class life that insists on ecclesial order and good relations with the wider society, and of an "early Catholicism" that espouses the threefold order of deacon, presbyter, and bishop.

While the theological emphasis of the Pastorals does differ from that of Paul's undisputed correspondence, it is an authentic development of the Pauline tradition that adapted Paul's theology to the new situation in which the Church found itself at the end of the first century. Moreover, since the Pastorals are addressed to pastors rather than communities of believers, it is not surprising that they deal with questions of order and office within the Church.

The Pastorals, however, are not solely concerned with questions of office and order, nor do they espouse a comfortable middle class way of life, as 2 Timothy shows when it summons Timothy to bear his share of suffering for the sake of the gospel. A careful reading of the Pastorals reveals that they contain a significant christology which develops the theme of God's appearance or epiphany in Christ. They also develop a rich moral teaching which draws an intimate connection between sound doctrine and the moral life. In a word, if preachers familiarize themselves with the Pastorals, they will find a fertile field from which they can reap a rich harvest.

Strategy: Understanding the Context

The historical context. If the Pastorals were not written by Paul, they were probably composed at the end of the first century by someone intimately familiar with the Pauline tradition, at a time when the Church in Asia Minor faced a serious threat from false teachers who were deviating from the gospel Paul had entrusted to the churches. Consequently, the author of the Pastorals writes in the name of his great teacher (a common practice in the ancient world) to remind church leaders of the Pauline tradition entrusted to them, and to instruct them how to oversee the congregations in their care. The Pastoral Epistles, then, might be viewed as pastoral handbooks.

As pastoral handbooks, the Pastorals instruct church officers to hold to the sound doctrine they have received, to transmit this teaching to faithful leaders who, in turn, must hand it on to other faithful leaders. Thus, the Pastorals are important for understanding what it means to guard the deposit of faith (1 Tim 6:20). This deposit of sound teaching originated with Paul who entrusted it to Timothy and Titus, who must now entrust it to other faithful witnesses. To assist Timothy and Titus in their work, Paul describes the qualifications for those who aspire to the office of bishop (1 Tim 3:1-7), deacon (1 Tim 3:8-13), and presbyter (1 Tim 5:17-23), as well as what seems to be an order of widows (1 Tim 5:9-16). In a word, the church of the Pastorals is in the process of structuring itself so that it can guard the rich deposit of sound teaching entrusted to it against false teachers (2 Tim 3:1-9).

The literary context. According to 1 Timothy, Paul left Timothy at Ephesus to oversee the church there when he went to the Roman province of Macedonia in Greece (1:3). To assist Timothy in this task, he charges him to carry out specific duties and instructs him to oversee the household of God, the Church. The letter alternates between sections in which Paul charges Timothy to act in a particular manner and sections in which he provides him with instruction for the household of God. The letter can be structured in this way:

> 1 Tim 1:3-20. Paul reminds Timothy of the original charge he gave him: to remain in Ephesus and "to instruct certain people not to teach false doctrines" (1:3). He then presents himself as the preeminent example of one in whom God's grace has been effective.

1 Tim 2:3-16. Having reminded Timothy of his original charge, Paul provides him with instruction for overseeing the household of God. In this section Paul describes the qualifications for bishops and deacons.

1 Tim 4:1-16. Paul renews his charge to Timothy and warns him of the false teaching that will disrupt the Church in the last days. Timothy must train himself for devotion and attend to the reading of the Scriptures.

1 Tim 5:1–6:2a. Paul provides Timothy with further instruction for the household of God. This instruction deals with widows, presbyters, and slaves.

1 Tim 6:2b-21. Paul gives Timothy a third and final charge. He is to pursue righteousness, devotion, and faith rather than riches, and he is to guard the rich deposit of faith that has been entrusted to him.

The manner in which this letter alternates between charge and instruction suggests that Timothy's ability to instruct and order the household of God requires faithfulness to the sound teaching entrusted to him.

The circumstances and tone of 2 Timothy are quite different from those of 1 Timothy. Paul is now in prison and must reckon with the prospect of death. Having suffered for the gospel, he exhorts Timothy to do the same. The letter, then, functions as Paul's last will and testament to his faithful co-worker, reminding him of what he (Paul) has taught and suffered, and encouraging him to follow his example. The letter consists of two exhortations and a solemn charge. It can be structured in this way:

2 Tim 1:6–2:13. Paul exhorts Timothy to bear his share of hardship for the gospel (1:8; 2:3) for which Paul is now suffering like a criminal (2:9).

2 Tim 2:14–3:9. Paul exhorts Timothy to stand fast in the face of false teaching that will surely come in the last days and has already made its appearance.

2 Tim 3:10–4:8. Paul reminds Timothy of his own suffering for the gospel and exhorts him to stand fast for the

sake of the gospel. Paul realizes that the time of his death is at hand. It is all the more important, then, that Timothy follow his example.

In reading 2 Timothy, one has the impression that the young Timothy may have been fearful because he faced the prospect of suffering for the gospel. Accordingly, Paul reminds him that he must bear his share of suffering. 2 Timothy, then, is a marvelous exhortation to ministers of every age who find themselves overwhelmed by the sufferings and trials entailed in preaching the gospel.

The Mercy of God
Twenty-fourth Sunday: 1 Tim 1:12-17

This reading occurs in the section that I have identified as Paul's first charge to Timothy (1:3-20). Its function within this section is to present Paul as an example of what God's grace can do in even the most sinful of persons. Accordingly, after charging Timothy to instruct certain people not to teach false doctrine (1:3-7) and identifying the kind of people who oppose sound teaching (1:8-11), Paul turns to the example of his own life. He was the foremost sinner because he blasphemed and persecuted the faith. However, he was treated mercifully because he acted in ignorance and unbelief. Consequently, he has become an example of the trustworthy saying, "Christ Jesus came into the world to save sinners" (1:15).

Identifying himself as the foremost sinner, Paul now understands that his conversion was part of a divine plan whereby God made him an example for all generations. Every sinner who contemplates the example of God's mercy toward Paul has reason for hope in that mercy. For, if God's mercy worked such wonders in the foremost of sinners, no sinner is beyond redemption or without hope.

Since the purpose of the gospel is to save sinners, Paul charges Timothy to instruct certain people not to teach false doctrine. Otherwise, the gospel will be perverted, and sinners will not be saved.

This text invites preachers to develop the theme of God's mercy in light of Paul's conversion. By presenting himself as the foremost of sinners, Paul shows that there is no limit to God's mercy. The God and Father of Jesus Christ is even merciful to those who blaspheme him. Indeed, this God is capable of making the greatest sinner the most outstanding example of his mercy.

Because he acknowledged his sinfulness, Paul was keenly aware of God's mercy toward him. When believers lose a sense of their sinfulness, they also lose their sense of God's mercy, for only those who have been forgiven understand what it means to receive mercy. Preachers will do well to remind their congregations that those who deny the presence of sin in their life ultimately deny themselves the experience of God's mercy.

Salvation for All
Twenty-fifth Sunday: 1 Tim 2:1-8

This reading belongs to the section I have identified as instructions for the household of God (2:1–3:16). In it, Paul requests prayers for those in authority because God wills that everyone be saved (2:1-7). He explains that he does not allow a woman to have authority over a man (2:8-15; a text which the Lectionary does not include). Next, he describes the qualifications for bishops and deacons (3:1-13). Finally he concludes with a poetic statement about the mystery of our religion (3:14-16). The nature of the material in this section is one of the reasons that some view the Pastorals as accommodating themselves to a comfortable middle-class faith that is primarily interested in a "quiet and tranquil life" (2:2). It would be a mistake, however, to interpret the material in this way.

While it is true that this section gives the impression of a church trying to find its place in society, it is hardly a church that is interested in a comfortable middle-class existence. Paul's reason for seeking a quiet and tranquil life is that the Church may be at peace to carry out God's will: that everyone be saved and come to the knowledge of the truth (2:3).

Paul then explains why God wills that all people be saved: there is only one God and one mediator, Jesus Christ, who gave himself as a ransom for all. Put another way, Paul affirms that God cares for all people no matter who they are, Gentile or Jew. In proclaiming that Christ Jesus is the one mediator between God and the human race, Paul affirms Christ's unique role in God's plan of universal salvation. In asking for prayers, then, he has a missionary intent: a quiet and tranquil life will provide the Church with an opportunity to preach the gospel of salvation to all.

Those who preach from this text will do well to reflect on its central message: that God "wills everyone to be saved and to come to knowledge of the truth" (2:4). While human beings are always too eager to put restrictions and limitations on who can be saved, God does not. God wills the salvation of all people; this is why Christ Jesus gave himself for all. Consequently, the Church must never define its mission too narrowly, as if some people were excluded. Nor can it minimize the significance of what Christ has done, as if Christ were one religious figure among many. The gospel is nothing less than God's offer of salvation for all people through Jesus Christ.

A Noble Confession
Twenty-sixth Sunday: 1 Tim 6:11-16

This text belongs to the section in which Paul gives his final charge to Timothy (6:2b-21). It begins with a warning about the danger of false teaching and the love of riches (6:2b-10) and concludes with an exhortation to the rich to rely on God rather than their wealth (6:17-19). Today's reading, which occurs between this warning and exhortation, warns Timothy of these things and exhorts him to pursue "righteousness, devotion, faith, love, patience, and gentleness" (6:11). It then charges him "to keep the commandments without stain or reproach until the appearance of our Lord Jesus Christ" (6:14). In charging Timothy to do these things, Paul reminds him of Jesus Christ's noble confession before Pontius Pilate, suggesting that the time has come for Timothy to follow this example.

A reading such as this indicates how faithful the Pastorals are to the Pauline tradition. For, while they seek a place for the Church in society, they do not merely encourage conformity to that society. Moreover, the Pastorals are keenly aware that Jesus Christ will appear again; consequently they remind believers that they must live with the eschatological tension that accompanies living between the resurrection and the final appearance of their blessed Savior.

This text will have special meaning for those who are ministers of the gospel since it calls them to imitate the noble confession that Christ made before Pontius Pilate. Inasmuch as all believers must make their own noble confession, Paul's words apply to them as well. Recalling Paul's charge to Timothy, preachers might give a similar charge to their own congregations, reminding them that believers will not find their fulfillment until the final coming of the Lord. As they wait for that glorious day, their task is to make a noble confession of their faith, as did Jesus before Pontius Pilate.

Sharing in the Hardship the Gospel Entails
Twenty-seventh Sunday: 2 Tim 1:6-8, 13-14

This reading comes from a section of 2 Timothy in which Paul exhorts his young assistant to bear his share of the hardship that the gospel entails (1:6–2:13). Since next week's reading comes from the final verses of this section (2:8-13), preachers should reflect on the entire section, even if they choose not to preach from this week's selection.

This week's section comes immediately after the letter greeting and thanksgiving (1:1-5) in which Paul recalls the sincere faith of Timothy's mother and grandmother, a faith which he is confident now lives in Timothy as well. Paul is in prison at Rome (1:17) for the sake of the gospel (1:8). Nearly everyone has abandoned him (1:15; 4:16), and he now suffers in chains as if he were a common criminal (2:9). Concerned that Timothy might become discouraged, Paul exhorts him "to stir into flame" (1:6) the gift he received when Paul imposed hands on him.

By imposing his hands on Timothy, Paul ordained him for service to the gospel and entrusted to him the sound teaching necessary for salvation which false teachers are now assaulting. Paul seems fearful that Timothy will be ashamed of him and the gospel which has brought him to such humiliating circumstances. Consequently, he exhorts Timothy to bear his share of hardship that the gospel entails (1:8; 2:3). Just as Paul is already suffering for the gospel, so Timothy must be prepared to do the same.

It is unfortunate that the Lectionary omits vv. 9-12 since they clarify what Paul means by the gospel: namely, God called us to a holy life not because of our works but because of his own design and the grace bestowed upon us in Christ Jesus from all eternity (1:9). That grace and design have been revealed in the appearance of Christ Jesus who destroyed death and brought life and immortality through the gospel. It is for this that Paul suffers. Because it is God's plan and grace, Paul is not ashamed of the gospel, and Timothy must be willing to bear his own share of the hardship that the gospel entails.

If Timothy has any doubt about how he is to behave, he should take as his norm the "sound words" (1:13) he heard from Paul. This sound teaching is the "rich trust" that Timothy must guard (1:14), and for which he must be prepared to suffer. To insure that this sound teaching will be handed on to the next generation, Timothy must entrust this teaching "to faithful people who will have the ability to teach others as well" (2:2).

The reading for this Sunday suggests several interrelated themes: bearing one's share of the hardship the gospel entails, not being ashamed of the gospel, guarding the sound teaching of the gospel that has been entrusted to the Church. Which theme the preacher focuses on will depend upon the circumstances of the congregation. For example, the preacher may need to remind a congregation that has become too comfortable with the world that authentic witness to the gospel entails hardship, and it must not compromise the rich deposit of sound teaching that has been entrusted to it. Whatever theme they choose, preachers will find a good starting point for their homily in the example of Paul who suffered as a common criminal for the sake of the gospel.

A Trustworthy Saying
Twenty-eighth Sunday: 2 Tim 2:8-13

This week's reading comes from the same section of 2 Timothy as did last week's (1:16–2:13), therefore preachers should read the text within its context. If they do, they will notice that immediately before this reading, Paul exhorts Timothy to entrust what he has heard from Paul to faithful people so that they will be able to teach others as well (2:2). Paul then repeats the refrain found in last week's reading, "Bear your share of hardship along with me like a good soldier of Jesus Christ" (2:3, see 1:8).

Having exhorted Timothy in this way, Paul recalls the gospel for which he suffers. It is the gospel about Jesus Christ, a descendant of David, who was raised from the dead. Because Paul has been faithful to this gospel, he has been chained as if he were a common criminal. However, these chains do not deter him, nor should they deter Timothy. For, even if the ministers of the gospel are in chains, the Word of God cannot be chained.

It is at this point that Paul introduces one of the many trustworthy sayings that occur throughout the Pastorals. The saying consists of four stanzas, the fourth of which breaks the pattern set by the first three.

> If we have died with him
>   we shall also live with him;
> if we persevere
>   we shall also reign with him.
> But if we deny him
>   he will deny us.
> If we are unfaithful
>   he remains faithful,
>   for he cannot deny himself (2:11-13).

The first two stanzas promise a recompense to believers who live in a particular way: if they die with Christ, they will live with him; if they persevere, they will reign with him. The third stanza then introduces a harsh warning: Christ will deny those who deny him. The fourth stanza, however, breaks this pattern. Thus, Paul does not say that if we are unfaithful, Christ will be unfaithful to us. For if Christ were unfaithful, he would deny his very self. Consequently, Paul concludes that Christ remains faithful even if we are unfaithful. Faithfulness is the defining characteristic of the Christ whom Paul preaches.

Those who preach from this text might focus on this faithful saying, especially its enigmatic ending that speaks of Christ's faithfulness. Most people will immediately understand the first three stanzas, but many will be puzzled by the last: if we are unfaithful, Christ will remain faithful. This final stanza, so different in form from the first three, is an opportunity to speak of Christ's faithfulness to his Father and to us. Most importantly, it offers believers a profound reason to remain faithful to the faithful Son of God.

Remain Faithful
Twenty-ninth Sunday: 2 Tim 3:14–4:2

This reading comes from a section of 2 Timothy in which Paul gives a final charge to his young assistant (3:10–4:8). The charge begins by recalling how Timothy has followed Paul's teaching and way of life and how Timothy has witnessed all the sufferings that Paul endured at Antioch, Iconium, and Lystra (3:10-11). Paul then notes that all who want to live a religious life in Christ Jesus will be persecuted. Thus Timothy must bear his share of the hardship that the gospel entails if he wishes to remain in Christ.

Having reminded Timothy how he has followed him thus far, Paul exhorts him to remain faithful to what he has learned and believed. Timothy can rely on this teaching because he knows who handed it on to him, and because he has been nurtured by the Scriptures since his youth. These Scriptures are the Sacred Scriptures of Israel which Paul describes as inspired and useful for teaching.

Having reminded Timothy of these things, Paul makes his solemn charge in 4:1. He summons Timothy to proclaim the word whether it is convenient or inconvenient since a time will come when people will no longer heed sound doctrine. Although the Lectionary reading concludes at 4:2, preachers should be aware that the whole charge consists of 4:1-8, and the final verses of the charge (4:6-8) will be used in next week's reading.

The section in which this reading is found (3:10–4:8) is the climax of 2 Timothy. The imprisoned Paul is now reckoning with his death, but before he dies he provides for the future of the Church he loves so dearly. Aware that false teachers have already infiltrated the household of God and led many astray, he solemnly charges Timothy to remain faithful to the teaching entrusted to him. If Timothy does this, then the sound teaching he learned from Paul will be handed on to the next generation.

This week's reading is an opportunity to remind the congregation of the important role it plays in handing on sound teaching to the next generation. Every generation plays an indispensable role in this process, and, if one generation fails to carry out its task, it will deprive the next of the sound teaching of the gospel. Paul's admonition, then, is meant for all believers, as well as for Timothy. Just as Paul exhorted Timothy to remain faithful and hand on the faith to the next generation, preachers must summon their congregations to do the same.

The End of the Race
Thirtieth Sunday: 2 Tim 4:6-8, 16-18

The first part of the reading (4:6-8) comes from the end of Paul's charge to Timothy, while the second (4:16-18) comes from the last section of the letter in which Paul describes his circumstances (4:10-16). In this last section, Paul portrays himself as having been deserted by nearly everyone except Luke in his hour of need. No one has come to his defense. Despite his circumstances, Paul affirms that the Lord stood by him and gave him strength. Paul is more confident than ever that Christ will rescue him again and bring him to "his heavenly kingdom" (4:18).

Paul compares his life to a race and himself to Christ's athlete. The race has involved suffering and persecution, but Paul has been faithful to Christ. Having finished the course, he now waits for the "the crown of righteousness" (4:8) that Christ will bestow upon him on the day of the parousia. That crown awaits all who faithfully run the race and long for the appearance of Christ Jesus.

By portraying himself in this way, Paul summons Timothy and all who read this letter to persevere in the race that is the

Christian life. Aware that those who have not finished the course can easily become discouraged, Paul offers himself as a model for Timothy and others to follow. His own life should encourage those who may be tempted to stop short of the finish line. Because he has run the race, Paul can assure them of what lies ahead.

This text is an opportunity to employ the metaphor of the race in order to explain the nature of the Christian life. Used as a metaphor, the race reminds believers that the Christian life requires perseverance, endurance, and hope of attaining the goal. Like runners in a long-distance race, believers will inevitably experience moments of exhaustion and disappointment, and even be tempted to quit the race. At other times they will temporarily lose sight of the goal and no longer be able to see the finish line. At these moments they must persevere and endure all the more, remembering the crown that awaits them: the righteousness that comes from God.

Strategy: Theological Themes

The Lectionary readings from the Pastoral Epistles focus on the importance of sound teaching, the need to hand this teaching on to the next generation, and the importance of bearing one's share of the hardship that the gospel entails.

The first two themes, the importance of sound teaching and the need to hand this teaching on to the next generation, should be familiar to Catholics acquainted with the theological concepts of the deposit of faith and the apostolic tradition. They are the kind of themes that need to be repeated to every generation since there is always a danger of compromising the faith. These themes, however, are most effectively preached when they are integrated with the third: the importance of bearing one's share in the hardship that the gospel entails. Sound teaching must be accompanied by a life which puts that teaching into practice. Those who call for sound teaching without sharing in the hardship the gospel entails will put into question the very teaching they propose.

2 Thessalonians

The Lectionary draws from 2 Thessalonians during the final weeks of Ordinary Time, a period during which the Church reflects on judgment, the second coming of Christ, and his kingship. Because Paul's teaching on the parousia is so prominent in this letter, it is an appropriate choice for the final weeks of the Church's liturgical year. However, since that teaching is also Paul's response to a particular problem within the Thessalonian congregation, preachers must be aware of the historical context and literary structure of this letter.

Strategy: Understanding the Context

The historical context. Many scholars question the Pauline authorship of 2 Thessalonians and categorize it, with Colossians, Ephesians, and the Pastorals, as one of the Deutero-Pauline letters. A reason for this judgment is the manner in which 2 Thessalonians presents the parousia. Whereas 1 Thessalonians argues that the Day of the Lord will come unexpectedly like a thief in the night (5:1-11), 2 Thessalonians lists the events which must occur before the Lord's coming (2:1-11). While it is important for preachers to be aware of this background, these scholarly opinions should not be the focal point of the homily.

2 Thessalonians presupposes that there has been a dramatic change in the situation of the Thessalonian congregation between the writing of 1 and 2 Thessalonians. In 1 Thessalonians, Paul addressed the following questions. What will happen to those who have died before the Lord's parousia? Will they share in his salvation, or will they be excluded because they died before the Lord's return? In response to these questions, Paul assures the Thessalonians that those who die in Christ will be raised at his coming. In 2 Thessalonians, however, the problem is different. The Thessalonians have received a letter or report to the effect that "the day of the Lord is at hand" (2:2). Consequently, some think that the Day of the Lord is about to take place or has already occurred. While Paul is confident that the parousia is near, he realizes that it has not taken place and

that it may not happen as quickly as some expect. Consequently, he must instruct the Thessalonians that the Day of the Lord has not yet arrived, and Christ will not return until certain events have taken place. To assist the Thessalonians, Paul explains what must happen before the parousia occurs (2:1-11).

The literary context. 2 Thessalonians begins with a greeting (1:1-2) and thanksgiving (1:3-12). The thanksgiving is especially important for understanding the letter since vv. 5-10 discuss the parousia. Accordingly, Paul assures the Thessalonians, who are undergoing a period of severe affliction, that God will repay with affliction those who are afflicting them, when Christ returns at his parousia. The emphasis on judgment and retribution in these verses is distinctive when compared with the description of the parousia in 1 Thess 4:13-18. Nonetheless, it makes eminent sense, given the situation of the afflicted Thessalonian community. They should endure their present circumstances because God will punish those who are now afflicting them.

After his greeting and thanksgiving, Paul turns his attention to the problem that must be addressed (2:1-12). The Thessalonians have heard a report, or received a letter supposedly from Paul, that the day of the Lord is at hand or has already occurred. Aware of this, Paul explains that the day of the Lord will not occur until certain events have taken place: a great apostasy and the appearance of "the lawless one" (2:3). At the present time, however, someone or something is restraining this lawless figure, and the parousia will not occur until the lawless one is released and makes his appearance. Only then will Christ return and destroy the lawless one. The Day of the Lord, then, is not as imminent as some mistakenly think, nor has it already taken place. Having resolved the main issue, Paul gives thanks that the Thessalonians have been chosen for salvation and requests their prayers (2:13–3:5).

In the final part of the letter, Paul deals with another problem (3:6-16). Some members of the community are leading disorderly lives. Instead of working for their living, they have become dependent on others. Accordingly, Paul encourages them "to work quietly and eat their own food" (3:12). We are not sure why these people acted as they did. Some commentators suggest that the disorderly were so convinced that the day of the Lord was at hand that they refused to work for their livelihood.

The letter concludes with a greeting (3:17-18) in which Paul assures the Thessalonians that *this* letter is from him.

When Will Christ Return?
Thirty-first Sunday: 2 Thess 1:11–2:2

The Lectionary reading for this week comes from the last part of Paul's thanksgiving (1:3-12) and the beginning of the body of the letter in which he deals with a false report that the day of the Lord is at hand (2:1-12). This choice of material for the Lectionary reading may make it difficult to preach from this text since the congregation will not have heard the whole of 2:1-12 in which Paul deals with the question of the parousia. Moreover, since the first part of the Lectionary reading (1:11-12) is used apart from the rest of the thanksgiving, the congregation will not have heard what Paul says about the parousia in 1:5-10. Therefore, those who preach from this text must place it within its literary context. More specifically, they must read the first part of the text (1:11-12) in light of the thanksgiving (1:3-11), and the second part of the text (2:1-2) must be read in light of the problem Paul discusses in 2:1-12. When this is done, the reading will afford preachers an opportunity to focus on the Second Coming of Christ.

2 Thessalonians makes two points about the Lord's parousia. First, it will be a day of judgment when God will vindicate his people (1:5-10). Accordingly, there is no need to lose hope in times of affliction, nor is there any need for believers to take vengeance into their own hands. Judgment belongs to God, and God will effect that judgment through Christ at the parousia. This is why Paul prays that God will make the Thessalonians "worthy of his calling and powerfully bring to fulfillment every good purpose and every effort of faith" (1:11). Second, though Paul is firmly convinced that the parousia is imminent, he knows that it will not occur until certain things have taken place (the great apostasy, the appearance of the man of lawlessness).

On first reading, it may seem that Paul is establishing a detailed time-table which enables believers to calculate exactly when Christ will return. Such time-tables, however, are common in the Bible, but their purpose is not to provide believers with a means of calculating the end, which nobody knows, not even the Son (Mark 13:32). Rather, they are meant to show that there is a divine plan that controls human history. The end will come soon, but only after certain things have taken place. When and how the end will occur is known to God alone.

This text provides preachers with an opportunity to proclaim a central article of Christian faith: Christ will come again. The question of most congregations, however, is when and how will Christ return? Will he come in our lifetime? Most believers would probably answer no. If Christ has not come in 2,000 years, why should he come in their lifetime? How will he come? On the clouds of heaven? Again, most believers probably understand that this is Biblical imagery which tries to express a transcendent reality in earthly terms. Accordingly, believers do not know *when* Christ will come or *how* he will return, but they firmly believe that he will come again in God's own way and in God's own time. The Second Coming of Christ will be the moment when God will effect salvation once and for all, when Christ will overcome every power of sin and earth. Aware that God's final salvation will not occur until Christ returns, the Church proclaims, "Christ will come again."

Mutual Prayer
Thirty-second Sunday: 2 Thess 2:16–3:5

This reading belongs to a section which functions as a second thanksgiving within the letter (2:13–3:16) in which Paul thanks God for choosing the Thessalonians "as the first fruits for salvation through sanctification by the Spirit and belief in truth" (2:13). The thanksgiving concludes with Paul praying for the Thessalonians (2:16-17) and requesting their prayers on his behalf (3:1-5). Within the letter, this material serves as a transition between Paul's discussion about the Day of the Lord (2:1-12) and the need for the disorderly to work and live quietly (3:6-16).

This is a difficult reading to preach from because it is a transitional text from one topic (the parousia) to another (the disorderly). Nonetheless, it suggests an important theme: the need for mutual prayer and support in the Christian life. Not only does Paul pray for the congregation (2:16-17), he requests their prayers on his behalf (3:1-5). In praying for the congregation (2:16-17), he describes God as the one who loves and gives encouragement and hope through his grace. In requesting the prayers of the congregation (3:1-5), he portrays God as faithful, the one who strengthens and guards us from the evil one.

Prayer is at the heart of the Christian life. Without it we cannot commune with God. By it, we are in communion with God and each other. The prayer Paul proposes here is prayer for each other which effects mutual support. Confident that the faithful God will strengthen and encourage those who entrust themselves to each other, Paul calls for the support that comes from praying for each other. Those who wish to preach from this text might reflect on what it means to pray for each other within the communion of saints.

Imitating Paul
Thirty-third Sunday: 2 Thess 3:7-12

In addition to the problem of the Day of the Lord, Paul addresses a second issue in 2 Thessalonians: the disorderly. For reasons we do not know, certain members of the community were living disorderly lives: "by not keeping busy but minding the business of others" (3:11). This disorderly conduct included an unwillingness to work and a dependency on others (3:10). Exactly why this occurred, we are not sure, but if some members of the community thought that the Day of the Lord was at hand, they may have decided that there was no need to work any more.

In response to this disorderly conduct, Paul presents himself as a model worthy of imitation. When at Thessalonica, he worked night and day so that he would not be a burden to the community. He provided for his own food and was not dependent on anyone. Paul's behavior is significant because he had a lively hope that the parousia would occur soon, perhaps in his own lifetime (1 Thess 4:15). Despite this hope, he carried on the daily affairs of life, working and supporting himself. His example teaches the Thessalonians to do the same.

Although this reading deals with a problem that is foreign to contemporary congregations, it is helpful for understanding how Paul lived between the time of Christ's resurrection and parousia. The resurrection of Christ assures him that the parousia is imminent. Because Christ has been raised from the dead (the first fruits of the general resurrection of the dead), Paul knows that the parousia can happen at any moment, even in his lifetime. Therefore, he lives in the world with hopeful expectation. His hope in Christ's imminent return does not, however, result in "dropping out," as if this world no longer had any meaning. Rather, he continues to work and support himself, as he lives in a world that is passing away.

Those who preach from this text might point to Paul's example to explain how contemporary Christians ought to live in the world. Living in an orderly manner means working quietly and supporting ourselves. As they do so, believers are keenly aware that the world they know is passing away, and God's final salvation may occur at any moment.

Strategy: Theological Themes

The readings of 2 Thessalonians are among the most difficult of the Lectionary to preach from because they do not allow congregations to hear all that Paul is saying. Their appearance at the end of the Church's liturgical year, however, suggests that preachers should develop the theological theme of the Day of the Lord. To do this effectively, they must reflect on the entire letter whose eschatological message can be summarized in this way: Although we do not know when Christ will come, we are confident that he will return in God's own time and in God's own way. When he does, God's salvation will be firmly and fully established. As we wait for that day, we live and work quietly in the world.

Conclusion

At the end of this book, it may be helpful to review the three strategies that I have proposed for those who preach from the Pauline readings of the Sunday Lectionary: (1) the historical and literary background of the text; (2) the context of the text; and (3) its theological themes.

The purpose of the first strategy was to enable preachers to understand the conversation between Paul and his churches. Paul did not write in a vacuum, nor did he compose theological treatises. Rather, his letters are responses to the problems and questions posed by the churches to which he ministered. Consequently, his theology is deeply pastoral inasmuch as it tries to resolve the problems of his congregations in light of the gospel that he preaches. When preachers understand Paul's pastoral technique, they will ask the right questions for preaching effectively; namely, what is the gospel saying here and now to this congregation? How does the gospel provide insight to the human situation? How can I respond to the needs of my congregation in light of what God has done in Christ? The gospel was Paul's guiding principle, and it must be the principle that guides preachers even today.

The purpose of my second strategy was to enable preachers to understand each text in light of its context since texts derive their meaning from a literary setting. One of the reasons that preachers find it so difficult to preach from Paul is that they do not understand his line of thought. Consequently, they are puzzled by the individual texts they encounter each week. The key to preaching Paul is understanding the structure of his argument and thought. When preachers do this, the individual parts of Paul's letters take on deeper meaning. The whole of the letter becomes the context for the individual text, enabling preachers to draw upon the full scope of Paul's theology. Preaching from Paul, then, requires planning and foresight. Instead of preaching as if each week were unrelated to what precedes and follows, preachers must look ahead and relate the Pauline readings to each other. For example, when the Lectionary reads from Romans or Galatians, preachers ought to read all of the texts well in advance and decide how they are related, and which texts they will preach from.

The purpose of my final strategy was to call attention to the theological dimension of Paul's writings. A pastor at heart, Paul was also a profound theologian, perhaps the most significant theological writer of the New Testament. He speaks of sin and redemption, life and death, faith and justification. More than any other writer of the New Testament, he draws out the implications of the Christ event for the moral life of believers. When preachers neglect Paul, their congregations are the poorer for it. Conversely, when they focus on the writings of this apostle, their congregations are enriched. Those who preach from the Pauline writings must wrestle with the thought of a profoundly religious thinker. They need not preach from Paul every week, but they should occasionally develop the great theological themes of his letters for the benefit of their congregations.

On most Sundays the homily will be drawn from the text of the gospel, and this is as it should be. But, from time to time, let the preacher preach from Paul as well.

Bibliography of Commentaries on the Pauline Letters and the Letter to the Hebrews

Romans

Achtemeier, Paul J. *Romans*. Interpretation: A Bible Commentary for Teaching and Preaching. Louisville: John Knox, 1985.

Byrne, Brendan. *Romans*. Sacra Pagina 6. Collegeville: The Liturgical Press, 1996.

Fitzmyer, Joseph A. *Romans: A New Translation with Introduction and Commentary*. The Anchor Bible 33. New York: Doubleday, 1993.

1 and 2 Corinthians

Best, Ernest. *Second Corinthians*. Interpretation: A Bible Commentary for Teaching and Preaching. Louisville: John Knox, 1987.

Collins, Raymond F. *First Corinthians*. Sacra Pagina 7. Collegeville: The Liturgical Press, 1999.

Hays, Richard B. *First Corinthians*. Interpretation: A Bible Commentary for Teaching and Preaching. Louisville: John Knox, 1997.

Lambrecht, Jan. *Second Corinthians*. Sacra Pagina 8. Collegeville: The Liturgical Press, 1999.

Murphy-O'Connor, Jerome. *1 Corinthians*. New Testament Message 10. Wilmington, Del.: Michael Glazier, 1982.

Scott, James M. *2 Corinthians*. New International Biblical Commentary: New Testament Series. Peabody, Mass.: Hendrickson, 1998.

Galatians

Dunn, James D.G. *The Epistle of the Galatians*. Black's New Testament Commentary. Peabody, Mass.: Hendrickson, 1993.

Martyn, J. Louis. *Galatians: A New Translation with Introduction and Commentary*. The Anchor Bible 33A. New York: Doubleday, 1997.

Matera, Frank J. *Galatians*. Sacra Pagina 9. Collegeville: The Liturgical Press, 1992.

Philippians

Craddock, Fred B. *Philippians*. Interpretation: A Bible Commentary for Teaching and Preaching. Louisville: John Knox, 1985.

Getty, Mary Ann. *Philippians & Philemon*. New Testament Message 14. Wilmington, Del.: Michael Glazier, 1980.

Martin, Ralph. *Philippians*. The New Century Bible Commentary. Grand Rapids, Mich.: Eerdmans, 1980.

Colossians, Ephesians, and Philemon

Bruce, F.F. *The Epistles to the Colossians, to Philemon, and to the Ephesians*. The New International Commentary on the New Testament. Grand Rapids, Mich.: Eerdmans, 1984.

Dunn, James D.G. *The Epistle to the Colossians and to Philemon*. The New International Greek Testament Commentary. Grand Rapids, Mich.: Eerdmans, 1996.

Mitton, C. Leslie. *Ephesians*. The New Century Bible Commentary. Grand Rapids, Mich.: Eerdmans, 1976.

Schnackenburg, Rudolf. *Ephesians: A Commentary*. Edinburgh: T.&T. Clark, 1991.

Schweizer, Eduard. *The Letter to the Colossians: A Commentary*. Minneapolis: Augsburg, 1982.

1 and 2 Thessalonians

Bruce, F.F. *1 & 2 Thessalonians*. Word Biblical Commentary 45. Waco: Word Books, 1982.

Marshall, I. Howard. *1 and 2 Thessalonians*. The New Century Bible Commentary. Grand Rapids, Mich.: Eerdmans, 1983.

Reese, James M. *1 and 2 Thessalonians*. New Testament Message 16. Wilmington, Del.: Michael Glazier, 1979.

Richard, Earl J. *First and Second Thessalonians*. Sacra Pagina 11. Collegeville: The Liturgical Press, 1995.

1 and 2 Timothy and Titus

Hanson, A.T. *The Pastoral Epistles*. The New Century Bible Commentary. Grand Rapids, Mich.: Eerdmans, 1982.

Karris, Robert J. *The Pastoral Epistles*. New Testament Message 17, Wilmington, Del.: Michael Glazier, 1979.

Knight, George W. *Commentary on the Pastoral Epistles*. New International Greek Testament Commentary. Grand Rapids, Mich.: Eerdmans, 1992.

The Letter to the Hebrews

Attridge, Harold W. *The Epistle to Hebrews*. Hermeneia: A Critical and Historical Commentary on the Bible. Philadelphia: Fortress, 1989.

Bruce, F.F. *The Epistle to the Hebrews: The English Text with Introduction, Exposition and Notes*. Grand Rapids, Mich.: Eerdmans, 1964.

Gench, Frances Taylor. *Hebrews and James*. Westminster Bible Companion. Louisville: Westminster John Knox, 1996.

Long, Thomas G. *Hebrews*. A Bible Commentary for Teaching and Preaching. Louisville: John Knox, 1997.

Index of the Pauline Readings
for the Sundays of Ordinary Time

Year A

Year B

Year C